TEAM LEADER'S
SURVIVAL GUIDE

Jeanne M. Wilson and Jill A. George, Ph.D.

McGraw-Hill

New York   San Francisco   Washington, D.C.   Auckland   Bogotá
Caracas   Lisbon   London   Madrid   Mexico City   Milan
Montreal   New Delhi   San Juan   Singapore
Sydney   Tokyo   Toronto

McGraw-Hill

A Division of The McGraw-Hill Companies

Copyright © 1997 by Development Dimensions International, Inc., Jeanne M. Wilson, and Jill A. George. All rights reserved. Printed in the United States of America. Except as permitted under the United States Copyright Act of 1976, no part of this publication may be reproduced or distributed in any form or by any means, or stored in a data base or retrieval system, without the written permission of the publisher.

3 4 5 6 7 8 9 0 QPD/QPD 9 0 2 1 0 9 8

ISBN 0-07-070893-2

Printed and bound by Quebecor/Dubuque.

McGraw-Hill books are available at special quantity discounts to use as premiums and sales promotions, or for use in corporate training programs. For more information, please write to the Director of Special Sales, McGraw-Hill, 11 West 19th Street, New York, NY 10011, or contact your local bookstore.

Table of Contents

Continued on next page ➤

Introduction

Today many leaders of teams feel lost at sea—unceremon-iously dumped overboard without a life preserver—as their organizations sail full speed ahead into self-directed teams.

The irony is that this usually is not due to any malicious intent by the organization. Unfortunately, top leaders of most organizations don't have any better ideas than you do about the changing role of the leaders in the transition to teams. While they may have a vision, they often don't know how to help you make that vision happen.

That's why this guide is designed as a self-coaching tool. It takes you through what you need to do week by week to plan, create, and sustain high-performance teams. It sets you up for success and helps you evaluate your progress.

This book is written directly to leaders of high-performance teams: self-directed teams, semi-permanent project teams, and empowered natural work teams. It doesn't matter whether you're leading a team of executives or a team of operators, whether you work in a service or a manufacturing organization—this guide is designed for you.

Mapping the Voyage

Most teams will go through three distinct phases in their development: Preteam, New Team, and Mature Team.

Preteam Phase

This phase begins when the organization first considers teams. It ends when teams are formally chartered and have held their first meeting. This first phase can last from 4 to 12 months. At the beginning of the Preteam Phase, leaders and employees hold their first discussions about empowered teams. By the end of this phase, everyone has a vision of what teams can accomplish, and you'll have a design for how teams will operate to turn that vision into a reality.

New Team Phase

The New Team Phase begins with the first team meeting and ends about 12 to 18 months later. In the beginning of this phase, you will spend a great deal of time getting your teams started by developing a team purpose (or mission) statement, goals, and clear roles and responsibilities. Shortly after start-up, you will spend 40 to 60 percent of your time coaching team members to handle responsibilities that used to be part of your old job, such as scheduling vacations, assigning daily tasks, and monitoring results. By the end of this phase, you will assume a few new tasks yourself, ranging from increasing involvement with larger business issues to more strategic technical projects.

Mature Team Phase

If your teams have been operating continuously for 12 months or more and are handling most of their new responsibilities successfully, you probably are in the Mature Team Phase. Certain key skills and behaviors distinguish mature teams from new teams: handling new responsibilities competently, solving interpersonal problems, working together willingly, and maintaining predictable levels of high performance. If these skills and behaviors are absent, your teams have not graduated to the Mature Team Phase.

Getting Your Bearings

This survey is designed to help you establish where you are in your team implementation. Are you in the Preteam Phase? The New Team Phase? Somewhere in the Mature Team Phase? To find out, complete the survey by checking the boxes for those statements that apply to your situation.

Preteam Phase

You are in the Preteam Phase if you're:

☐ Becoming aware of the need to change.

☐ Completing a readiness assessment to determine your organization's cultural strengths and developmental areas.

☐ Defining organizational values to drive behaviors toward a more empowered culture.

☐ Still not sure that teams will work.

☐ Responding to skeptics who are wary of the team concept.

☐ Unsure about what your new role will be.

☐ Reconfiguring roles and responsibilities at all levels so people have more decision-making ability.

☐ Redesigning departmental boundaries so teams can control errors or variances within their own boundaries.

☐ Focusing on your personal needs and role.

If six or more of these statements apply to you, you're probably in the Preteam Phase. Pages 1 through 77 will be particularly helpful as you form teams. However, if you think you are beyond the Preteam Phase, you still might want to skim the activities to see if there is anything you and the team should do to become even stronger.

New Team Phase

You are in the New Team Phase if you're:

☐ Helping team members work together within new organizational boundaries.

☐ Transferring responsibilities to team members according to an Empowerment Schedule.

☐ Developing team goals in alignment with your organization's vision and values.

☐ Struggling not to revert to the comfort of your old role, especially during crises or when faced with technically complex problems.

☐ Spending 40 to 60 percent of your time coaching and developing team members.

☐ Seeing attitudes and behaviors becoming aligned with the team concept.

☐ Looking for more information to share with your teams about customer complaints, profitability, and related business matters.

☐ Focusing more on your teams' needs and roles than on your own needs and role.

As a rule, you're in the New Team Phase if six or more of these items apply to you. Pages 79 through 231 will help you move successfully into the next phase: Mature Teams.

Mature Team Phase

If your teams have been operating continuously for 12 to18 months and are handling most of their new responsibilities successfully, you're probably in the Mature Team Phase. You are in the Mature Team Phase if you're:

☐ Spending up to 80 percent of your time on strategic customer or product and service improvements.

☐ Working with teams that handle their new responsibilities successfully.

☐ Coaching teams to assume more advanced responsibilities, such as budgeting, peer review, and salary increases.

☐ Watching your teams produce at peak levels.

☐ Maintaining quality levels at an all-time high.

☐ Noticing that doubts about the team concept have practically disappeared.

☐ Stretching to take on roles outside your department or facility.

You've made it to the Mature Team Phase if at least five of these items apply to you. Pages 233 through 283 will help you maintain your high-performance teams.

The Journey

This book is designed to be a user-friendly, month-by-month planning guide to help you successfully navigate through each of the three team implementation phases.

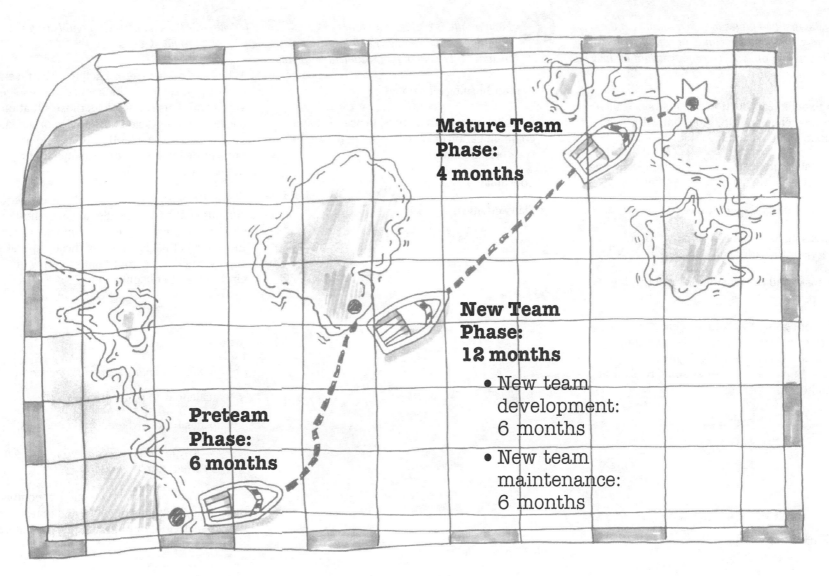

Mature Team Phase: 4 months

New Team Phase: 12 months

- New team development: 6 months
- New team maintenance: 6 months

Preteam Phase: 6 months

How the Guide is Organized

The phases are presented in monthly segments, with each month containing the following components:

 The first two pages for each month set the stage for what you can expect to discover in the month ahead. These pages feature two main sections:

What to Expect: This section highlights certain aspects of the changing situation that will affect what you do and how you do it. For instance:

- Team members' current information, coaching, development, and empowerment needs.

- Team members' expectations.

- Changes in your role as you move from supervisor to leader and coach.

- New tasks and responsibilities you need to prepare for.

Possible Concerns: As your role changes, each month brings new questions, challenges, and uncertainties. This section highlights a few common examples and provides some reassuring advice on how to proceed.

 Each month is divided into four planning/action weeks. Each week includes a variety of tools that will help you:

- Answer burning questions.

- Establish new relationships, processes, and communication channels with people inside your organization.

- Coordinate resources for team members.

- Plan activities.

- Chart progress.

 At the end of each monthly segment, you're provided with:

When to Call for Help: Each month presents new challenges, some of which you can't resolve on your own. This section lists those situations and suggests whom to go to for advice or guidance: your manager, peers, other team leaders, other units or departments, or team members themselves.

If You Do Nothing Else . . . : Progress requires commitment and work. So, if you do nothing else each month, make sure you complete or satisfy the items in this list. Letting these imperatives slip by could leave your teams floating in circles in a sea of confusion.

 Each monthly segment concludes with:

- A calendar to plan activities.

- Spaces to record monthly outcomes:

    —Key lessons learned: What worked and what didn't work.

    —Your personal time budget (comparing actual times to suggested times spent on activities, and calculating the differences.)

How to Use This Guide

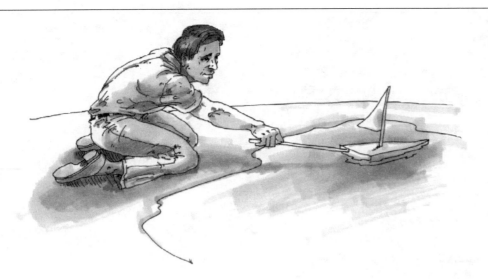

On Your Own

After you pinpoint where you and your teams are in the team continuum (Preteam, New Team, or Mature Team), you might want to skim the entire guide. This will give you an idea of what to expect and will help you recognize when you or your teams are grappling with an issue that is addressed elsewhere in the guide.

Many leaders find it helpful to set aside a specific time each week (such as 9:30 a.m. Monday) to work through that week's prescribed issues, exercises, and activities. In most cases this review will take about half an hour.

In a Group

Some organizations used an early version of this guide as the weekly agenda for supervisory self-help groups. Each week, one leader would take responsibility for facilitating a discussion of the issue outlined for that week, helping the group apply it to their own specific situations. You too can follow this format or adopt some other method that best addresses your situation.

Hint

Although the guide is laid out in a sequential format, we recognize that teams do not develop in a lock-step manner. For this reason, we suggest that you use the guide as a menu from which to select activities that are appropriate for you and your teams' development diet.

Notes. . .

Preteam Phase

Welcome to the Preteam Phase! The following pages will help you become familiar with (and start addressing) some of the important issues you and your employees will face in the transition to teams. Here is a month-by-month, week-by-week look at the Preteam Phase:

Month 1

- What are empowered teams?
- Show me the results
- Getting up to speed
- Understanding the organization's vision

Month 2

- Checkpoint #1: Synchronizing your vision
- Conducting a "stay-tuned" meeting
- Preparing the case for change
- Identifying what's in it for everyone

Month 3

- Communicating the case for change
- Redesigning for results
- Do-it-yourself redesign
- Changing your role's focus: From microscope to telescope

Month 4

- Preparing for your new role
- Time management for team leaders
- How to assess progress
- Building your employees' skills

Month 5

- Increasing employee horsepower: Building skills—continued
- No guts, no glory: Sharing your leadership responsibility
- Increasing your own horsepower: Leadership skills
- Checkpoint #2: Finalizing your role with your manager

Month 6

- Dealing with performance problems
- Navigating with a skeptical crew
- Trust must come first
- Checkpoint #3: Reviewing progress

Preteam Month 1

Notes. . .

Month 1

What to Expect

You and other people in the organization will spend a lot of time planning how work teams will be set up and how they will function. Occasionally you might feel as if this preparation is a waste of your time. Don't let feelings of frustration or impatience force you off course. Planning is important; stick with it. Failure to plan is one of the major reasons why team implementations fail (Wellins, Byham, and Wilson, 1990).

Agreeing on the Vision

Early in the Preteam Phase people might be confused and in disagreement about the definition of self-directed teams, how far the organization is going, or even why the organization would use teams as a vehicle for organizational improvement. This lack of vision is common in team implementation efforts. Don't worry too much about disagreements and misunderstandings. They are natural at this time. Discussing them and asking questions will lead to a common understanding. Once there is general agreement and understanding of where the organization is going with teams, progress becomes easier.

Importance of Limits

Moving to empowered teams does not mean that you, the organization, or its employees can stock the fleet with every kind of ocean-going luxury or want-to-have. The sky is not the limit. Rather, the move to empowered teams should be a carefully planned, rational transformation. It should create—within clearly defined and understood limits—a better equipped, more responsive, and productive workforce. Knowing the plans and boundaries for the implementation of teams will go a long way toward clarifying everyone's responsibilities and expectations.

Possible Concerns

I've heard a lot of talk around here about teams lately, and I have major doubts about whether teams would really work here.

You're not alone in wondering if work teams can be successful in your organization, with your union, or with your managers. However, you should be reassured to learn that work teams have proven successful in all types of settings—sales organizations, start-ups, retrofits, unionized organizations, government agencies, chemical processing plants, hospitals, distribution centers, and more. The kind of industry, business, or operation is less important than working together to lay a solid foundation on which effective teams can be built.

What exactly will my role be?

At the start of the Preteam Phase, it's difficult to specify exactly how each leader's role will change. At this point team structure and responsibilities have not taken shape. And while the leader's role is a key component to the team design, that design usually isn't completed until four to five months into the Preteam Phase. In time you will be doing less firefighting and more consulting, people development, or special projects. In fact, most leaders find that their roles eventually take a major turn: Where once they spent half their time on paperwork, after team implementation leaders find that they spend that time coaching or working on special projects. A key to re-creating your role to ensure future success is to get involved early on in redefining how that role will change.

Your Focus This Month

This month you will need to work on the following areas as you prepare to launch into teams:

- Learning what empowered teams are and what they do.

- Understanding how self-directed teams are different from other kinds of teams.

- Identifying sources of information about empowered teams.

- Understanding your organization's vision and what it means to your area in the future.

Week 1

What are empowered teams?

History

Empowered teams (such as self-directed teams) are not new. Permanent work groups that control their day-to-day production, quality, and administrative duties have been getting results since at least the early 1940s. Work teams were first established in British coal mines. However, it wasn't until the 1970s that work teams started to catch on in North America. Currently, more than 30 percent of the organizations in the United States have self-directed teams in some part of their operations.

The Basics

Empowered teams are formed because they produce both technical results (increased productivity, better quality, and reduced cycle time) and social improvements (ownership of the work, increased responsibility, and collaboration between work areas). The secret to getting these results lies in the design of the teams' work flow and responsibilities. The most effective teams control their work from start to finish, as the illustration shows.

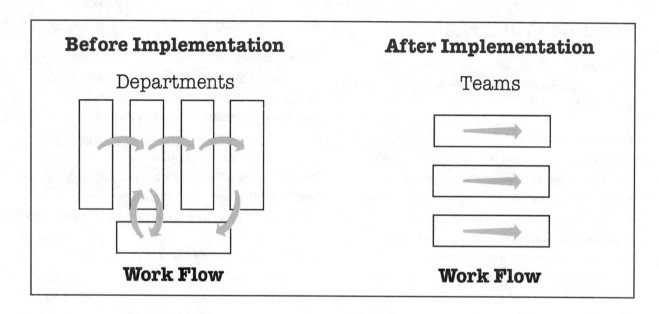

Before Implementation

Departments

Work Flow

After Implementation

Teams

Work Flow

Empowered teams typically solve the problems listed below. Check those that apply to you.

Delays

☐ Machine downtime

☐ Waiting on lab results

☐ Delays for maintenance

☐ Waiting for data or reports

☐ Equipment installation

☐ Layers of approval

☐ Late shipments

☐ Delays in changing equipment

☐ Delays in solving customers' problems

☐ Long cycle times

☐ Extended patient stay

Errors

☐ Reworking errors in reports

☐ Inaccurate customer orders

☐ Errors handed from department to department

☐ Defective supplies

☐ Product does not adhere to customers' specifications (scrap)

People Problems

☐ Spending time on conflicts between departments

☐ Lack of motivation

☐ Blaming others

☐ No variety in jobs

☐ Underutilized skills

☐ Lack of understanding of overall business

With guidance and coaching from you, your teams can find ways to eliminate these delays, avoid these errors, and solve these people problems.

Week 2
Show me the results

It's clear: Self-directed teams (SDTs) outperform other types of teams. One study of more than 130 organizations found that when teams are designed around a start-to-finish, multifunctional work system—and people share leadership tasks—the financial and quality results are significantly better than when project teams or work groups are formed within traditional departments (Macy, 1993). A study by John Cotter (1983) revealed these results for organizations with SDTs:

- 93 percent improved productivity

- 86 percent decreased operating costs

- 86 percent improved quality

What empowered teams could mean to your organization:

Organization	Results
Sandpaper manufacturer	*Twenty-five percent greater productivity in redesigned self-directed distribution teams.*
Manufacturer of hand tools	*A redesigned load chain team saved the company $180,000 during the first month.*
Insurance company	*A 75 percent improvement in case processing time.*
Research and development company	*Reduced cycle time from three months to three weeks on a product line.*
Chemical packaging company	*Increased productivity plantwide by 18 percent.*
Financial services company	*Processes 800 lease applications a day—twice the amount in the traditional structure.*
Beer manufacturer	*Fifty percent reduction in beer waste.*
Asian semiconductor manufacturer	*A $50 million savings over 10 years from quality improvements.*
Manufacturer of polymer emulsions	*Reduced the new product development cycle at one plant from five years to nine to ten months.*
Maker of complex radiotherapy accelerators	*Cut manufacturing costs by 22 percent over five years.*

Some facts about teams:

- SDTs outperform natural work teams and project teams.

- The average SDT achieves bottom-line results in three to five years.

- The secret to those results is the work-flow design and the amount of shared leadership.

What kind of results are important to you?

Write some targets for your job or department, then briefly describe a possible goal for that target. An example is included.

Target	Possible Goal
Reduce cycle time	*By 20 percent*

Week 3
Getting up to speed

Your first step is to understand how empowered teams work, how they might be different from the way you work now, and how they are typically implemented. The following list includes several ideas for how you can increase your knowledge about teams and, in the process, learn how your role will be affected and improved by the move to teams.

Visit or contact someone in an organization with teams. (This approach to learning provides a lot of information effectively; however, it might be difficult to do. Some organizations are set up to handle such visits, for which they charge a small fee. At least consider holding a telephone conference call with representatives from these organizations.)

- Saturn Corporation, Springhill, TN, an automobile manufacturer

- Hannaford Brothers, Schodack Landing, NY, a retail supermarket and food distributor

- Corning, Greenville, OH

- Eastman Chemical Co., Kingsport, TN

Attend conferences on teams.

- The Ecology of Work Conference (603-942-8189)

- The International Conference on Self-managed Work Teams (817-565-2653)

- Association for Quality and Participation (513-381-1959)

Watch videos about organizations with teams.

- "Topeka Pride" (Call Blue Sky Productions, 215-844-4444.)

- "The Rolm and Haas Story" (Call Blue Sky Productions, 215-844-4444.)

- "The Leadership Alliance" with Tom Peters (Call Video Publishing House, 800-824-8889.)

Read books, articles, or case studies about teams.

- *Empowered Teams* (Richard S. Wellins, William C. Byham, Jeanne M. Wilson)

- *Inside Teams* (Richard S. Wellins, William C. Byham, George R. Dixon)

- *All Teams Are Not Created Equal* (Lyman D. Ketchum, Eric Trist)

- *Business Without Bosses* (Charles Manz, Henry Sims)

- *Succeeding as a Self-directed Team* (Ann Harper, Bob Harper)

- *Leadership Trapeze* (Jeanne M. Wilson, Jill George, Richard S. Wellins, William C. Byham)

- *Succeeding With Teams* (Richard S. Wellins, Dick Schaaf, and Kathy Harper Shomo)

An effective way to increase your knowledge and understanding about teams, and to share that knowledge with others, is to create an in-house book club. Regularly schedule readings, with others in your group, of interesting and pertinent chapters, articles, or entire books from the list above. Discuss what you've read over lunch or at a regularly scheduled meeting. Use the next page to keep track of ideas generated by your reading, discussions, or site visits.

Valuable lessons about: Employees My role My manager's role	**How can I apply this to my organization?**
Issues to avoid around: Employees My role My manager's role	**How can I help my department avoid these problems?**

Week 4

Vision—A Definition

A vision is a statement of the desired future. It routinely contains a nonnumerical financial goal and a description of the organization's or unit's strategic advantage, all in a way that inspires employees.

Now that your organization is about to implement empowered teams, you need to understand its plans or vision for that implementation in detail. Understanding the organization's vision—and helping other employees understand that vision—has several benefits:

For you, understanding the organization's vision will:

- Prepare you to answer questions about the move to teams.

- Give you an idea of what to expect in your own role.

- Give you a context for discussing the changes or decisions that result from the move to teams.

For your employees, understanding the vision will:

- Clear up any confusion they have about where the company is heading.

- Explain their opportunities for growth and satisfaction in the future.

- Help them feel that they are taking an active part in the larger business.

Creating a Vision

Most organizations use a two-pronged approach to implementing teams. One prong is the steering team, consisting of top managers representing several areas or functions in the organization. The steering team focuses on the *what* of the team implementation; that is, they develop the vision for the implementation. From managers, supervisors, support professionals, and employees, the organization forms the second prong: the design team. This group builds on the vision and plans *how* the team vision will be implemented.

A vision is more than a paragraph in a fancy frame. A vision should give you a sense of how far you want to go—and how fast. It should help clarify management's expectations, especially in terms of how everyone's behavior in the "new team world" will differ from the current world.

Review the following items to understand what a vision is and how it can work for you and your employees during the team implementation. Ask yourself, What pieces of the vision do I have now and what do I need to work on with my group?

1. Following is an example of a **vision statement** that people can understand and remember:

   We make Quality happen. . . . To be the dominant and most successful company in the market we serve, beyond all competition. Achieving that mission will require a company-wide focus on the same set of operating values.

2. **Values**—corporate, departmental, and individual—support the organization's vision because they determine how work is done and how people interact. Values often are defined by specific behavioral practices. These "best practices" answer the question, What do these values mean and what do they have to do with me? For example, the value "empowerment" might be defined by these best practices:

   • Decisions are made at the lowest appropriate level.

   • Financial information is shared at all levels.

   • Employees who accept responsibility and ownership are rewarded.

3. An **Empowerment Schedule** that shows how far your teams will go—and how fast—is a good tool for promoting understanding about teams. The schedule clarifies people's expectations. For example, after the start-up, teams should be working on these tasks:

Empowerment Schedule

3 months	6 months	9 months	12 months
• Develop and coordinate a cross-training plan. • Coordinate getting operational safety equipment on the floor. • Handle vacation scheduling. • Assign tasks to members.	• Coordinate time and attendance with human resources. • Run shift overlap meetings. • Review customer feedback as a team.	• Set team goals based on the organization's goals. • Call for materials and maintenance directly.	• Select new team members. • Coordinate the preventive maintenance plan.

Continued on next page

4. Your teams should be focused on achieving organizational goals. Consider what those goals might be while reading these examples:

- *Reduce recordable accidents from eight to three.*

- *Increase employee development by ensuring 100 percent level of operation literacy.*

- *Reduce length of patient stay from five days to four days this year.*

5. Establish guidelines for how teams will be implemented. Guidelines define limits and expectations. One group came up with these questions to help it set guidelines and understand the impact of the team implementation on its work:

How or when can teams:

- *Purchase or move equipment?*

- *Add additional staff?*

- *Expect to see their compensation aligned with increased decision making?*

- *Work overtime on team projects?*

Basic Vision Questions

Because it covers so much territory, the vision statement sometimes is misunderstood or can be difficult to translate into concrete actions. Answering the questions on page 13 will help you attach real meaning to the vision statement. Review the suggestions provided under "Sources" and "Useful answer" to generate ideas. Note your organization's information in the space provided.

Question 1: Why teams and why now?

Sources: Team's champion, steering committee

Useful answer: Our quality teams have produced impressive results, but they still are viewed as an extracurricular activity. We need a permanent vehicle for employees to become more empowered because two competitors have lower costs than ours. We all have access to the same technology. Our only advantage is our people.

My organization's information:

Question 2: Who's sponsoring the team?

Sources: Your manager, steering committee

Useful answer: In our organization we believe it's important that the change has many champions. All steering committee members are champions or drivers of the implementation. That way, the vision will live beyond any one person.

My organization's information:

Question 3: What are management's expectations of teams?

Sources: Your manager

Useful answer: We believe that XYZ's first team will begin officially in April and that 100 percent of the employees will be in teams within two years. Our hope is that XYZ teams will be handling their own scheduling, tracking, and training.

My organization's information:

Notes. . .

Month 1

When to Call for Help

- If you can't get information on the difference between empowered teams and other forms of employee involvement, and if your sponsor can't explain why teams will improve your business. Meet with other supervisors and your manager to clarify these topics. It's important that everyone understands these topics before moving forward.

- Definitely ask for assistance from someone with experience before you decide to skip any steps in the team implementation process.

If You Do Nothing Else . . .

1. Educate yourself on work teams. Learn why organizations are moving to self-directed teams, how teams are implemented, their common traps, and how "teamwork" (collaboration) differs from "working in teams" (workers responsible for production, quality, and leadership tasks). Read about teams and attend team training workshops and conferences.

2. Start thinking about changes now and involve your employees in discussions about what those changes should be. Results won't happen without fundamental change. But you don't have to reinvent the wheel. Look at how other organizations are achieving results by changing their fundamental processes and systems. Learn the best of their systems.

3. Include the union leader in your area in your education efforts.

Month at a Glance

MONDAY	TUESDAY	WEDNESDAY	THURSDAY	FRIDAY	SATURDAY/SUNDAY
			Ask my department to read an empowered teams book	Read an empowered teams book —1 hour	
	Read an empowered teams book —2 hours			Discuss the empowered teams book with the department —30 minutes	
	Request authorization to visit an organization with teams		Prepare some site visit questions —1 hour		
				Ask my department what they think are our biggest delays —30 minutes	

Time Budget

	Goal	Actual
Team coaching	10%	
Project work	10%	
Administrative	70%	
Personal development	10%	

Key Lessons

_____

_____

_____

_____

_____

_____

Next Steps

_____

_____

_____

_____

_____

Preteam Month 2

Notes. . .

Month 2

What to Expect

You are preparing to explain the organization's vision—but your employees want to know exactly who will be doing what, when, and in what team! They want more detail than you can supply, and they have more questions than you can answer right now. It's okay to say, "I don't know. But I can tell you when we should have information on that." Telling people that you can't answer their questions right away but that you are working on finding the answers goes a long way to building trust, an essential element of a successful team implementation.

Some leaders use the analogy of constructing a new office building as a way to explain what's happening now. They will say, "At this point we know we need more space. We've turned the issue over to an architect (the design team), but we haven't seen the plans yet."

Providing Business Focus

Often business information passes from the manager to the supervisor and stops there. One of your new responsibilities is to make sure you discuss your organization's business—its customers, goals, expectations—with your employees. Business focus will help motivate your employees to change and keep your implementation focused on bottom-line issues. As you share more business information (costs, news about the competition, sales backlogs, and customer requirements) with your employees, they will be better able to make effective decisions.

Managing Expectations

One of the most important things you will need to do when starting empowered work teams is to manage expectations—yours, your employees', and your manager's. Be realistic about what your group can accomplish.

One hospital leader said keeping everyone's expectations realistic is like a trip to the grocery store. If you go without a budget (limits), you will end up buying expensive treats you don't need. On the other hand, if you go in with a budget and a list (a plan), you leave the store only with what you really need. Your job is to help everyone stay within their "expectation budget" in the move to teams.

Possible Concerns

You don't know the people I work with. Half of them don't want more responsibility and the other half couldn't handle it.

In some cases this is a legitimate concern. Other times, however, it's merely an excuse people use to avoid handing off tasks to teams. In every organization employees want more responsibility than their managers give them credit for. It's up to you to make sure they have the information, reassurance, and training they need to handle new responsibilities successfully. Make sure you:

- Give employees the big picture of the shift to teams so they can understand why change is necessary, what changes are being made, and why these changes are important.

- Show them that you have accepted the case for change.

- Help employees tackle new tasks by assuring them you will provide the resources (that is, advice, information, training, etc.) they need to succeed.

- Show them what's in it for them.

If I'm about to discuss our organization's vision for teams, how do I handle the Chicken Little's ("the sky is falling") and the naysayers?

Every leader is going to have to deal with people who initially resist change. Do the following:

- Listen to people's issues and concerns and show that you understand them. Many people ask tough, targeted questions as a way to test your understanding and increase their own understanding. They are not necessarily resistant. Most adults learn by challenging ideas and assumptions.

- Share examples, stories, and information. You can increase your chances of winning them over to your point of view if you ask for their help in understanding how the changes could work.

- Ask questions! Asking questions often is more effective than "sell-sell-sell" in getting people's interest and commitment to change.

What if I'm not sold 100 percent myself?

At this point you don't have to be. Showing that you're thinking through team implementation issues will let employees and managers know that you're trying to be practical and realistic. However, if you believe that work teams are not beneficial for you or your employees, identify your concerns. Research topics related to those concerns, either through visits to organizations with teams or reading. Open yourself up to new ways of doing things. Don't skip or second guess implementation steps until you have all the facts.

Your Focus This Month

This month you will focus your efforts on:

- Checking with your manager.

- Conducting a "stay-tuned" meeting.

- Preparing your employees for change.

- Discussing what benefit the change will have for everyone.

Week 1
Checkpoint #1: Synchronizing your vision

You and your manager should agree on what the organization's vision for teams means to you and your employees. Together, review the vision, then discuss these questions and any others you might have. Take notes in the space provided.

Implementation in My Area

- When will teams start and when will my area become involved officially?

- What can my department do now to get in sync with the rest of the organization?

Budgeting Time for Teams

- Typically, I'll need at least 15 percent of employees' time each week to explain the vision, build awareness and skills, etc. Is this doable?

My Development

- How much time can I devote to learning team basics and communicating the vision to employees this month? During the first two months, I'll need about two hours a week to address these issues. Also, I'll spend about 50 percent of my time coaching and teaching and 10 percent on personal development.

Involvement in Team Design

- How can I be involved in shaping the design?

- How much time can I devote to team design and implementation?

Motivating Yourself: Career Options

During the team implementation your role probably will change into one that is more strategic and proactive or one that is more technical (as a consultant). To motivate yourself, talk with your manager about a career options learning path now. Leaders who set a two- or three-year career goal will find that their teams will become self-directed more quickly. Use the form on page 19 to discuss your career path with your manager. ➤

Possible Career Paths	Skills I Need	How Can I Develop These Skills?
• Special project work with external suppliers, customers, or new team installations. This path's appeal:	For special projects: • Building business partnerships • Communication skills, such as active listening • Customer service skills	
• Technical project leader. This path's appeal:	For leading technical projects: • Managing incoming work • Sponsoring process improvements • Setting goals and tracking progress • Knowledge of the work process • Project management • Proposal development	
• Staff work in another area, such as human resources, purchasing, engineering, or planning. This path's appeal:	For working in other areas: • Knowledge of the area's analysis and tactical steps • Knowledge of computer support system • Knowledge of legal issues related to work in staff area • Knowledge of best practices for chosen area	
• Team consultant/coordinator. This path's appeal:	To consult with teams: • Team facilitation skills • Organizational change and work team implementation • Team implementation models • Basic consulting, such as diagnosing organizational problems, project planning, progress assessment, and coaching key leaders	

Career option agreements my manager and I made:

Week 2
Conducting a "stay-tuned" meeting

By now your employees know that change is on the way. You need to develop their buy-in to the move to teams. In a staff meeting tell them what you know about teams and what the organization wants to do with the team implementation. Make it clear that this is an informational meeting and that they should "stay tuned" for more details. Cover these topics:

- A description of empowered teams and how they build on or are different from the current operation.

- Common results of teams.

- Average length of time it takes for an SDT to become fully functioning.

- Upcoming communications on your organization's vision and how teams will achieve that vision.

Sample Agenda

This sample agenda includes time to answer employees' questions. Add to or revise it to fit your special needs.

8:30	*Statement of purpose: to start the process of building support for the team implementation by sharing information about the organization's direction with teams*
8:45	*Description of self-directed teams*
9:00	*Common results of SDTs*
9:15	*Examples of SDTs in our industry*
9:30	*How long does it take to implement teams?*
9:45	*More details on the company's vision for teams in three weeks*
10:00	*Conclude meeting*

Make sure your agenda includes the points covered in Preteam Month 1. Complete the statements below and list other points you want to make.

- Self-directed teams outperform other types of employee involvement by:

- Other companies in our industry with successful teams are:

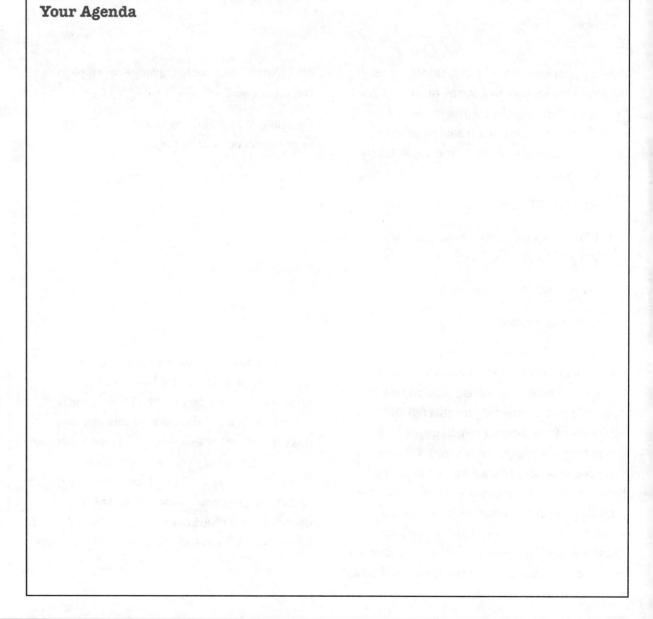

Your Agenda

Week 3
Preparing the case for change

Building your employees' commitment to the transition begins with motivating them to change. People are motivated by many factors. But you'll need to take four steps to create the employee motivation needed to result in successful teams. You will explain:

1. Internal and external business pressures.

2. Where the organization is now and where it wants to go.

3. What's in it for us as teams?

4. What can we expect next?

First, you need to make your employees aware of the pressures your organization is facing both internally (competition among departments, operating costs, expected growth, etc.) and externally (new customer requirements, competitor advantages, regulations, etc.). Second, you need to be able to discuss the difference between where the organization is now and where it needs to be in the future if it's to remain a competitive player in the market or industry. Third, you need to answer questions about how all employees and the union (if applicable) will benefit from the change.

And, fourth, you have to explain what employees can expect next with the change.

Question: Which of these four steps will have the most impact on your employees?

To be able to discuss topics 1 and 2, gather information during the next two weeks on organizational and departmental key business indicators. These indicators prepare you to discuss each of the four topics. The worksheet on the next page, or one you create, will help you collect the necessary data. Refer to your own reports or go to your finance or quality departments for the information you don't have on hand. Topics 3 and 4 will be addressed next week.

Motivating a Giant

If you think your task is impossible, consider the situation of a federal tax return processing center. The employees in this major government bureaucracy needed to be convinced that change was necessary. They were motivated to commit to the change when they learned that the number of tax returns to be processed would grow significantly in coming years. Also, as tax laws changed, claim processing would become even more complex. They just couldn't continue processing returns in the same old way if the taxpaying public's needs were to be met.

Our Business—Now and in the Future

Use the chart on page 23 (or one like it) to identify the basic business information you need to create motivation for change among your employees.

➤

Business Indicators	Organization		Department	
	Now	Future (vision/goal)	Now	Future (vision/goal)
• Percent of on-time delivery				
• Percent of orders completed				
• How often we meet customer requirements				
• In-house cycle time to complete an order				
• Number of units shipped				
• Operating costs				
• Percent of employees cross-trained				
• Employee satisfaction/morale				
• Others				

Week 4
Identifying what's in it for everyone

Before you discuss with your employees specific details about your organization's move to teams, you need to prepare an answer to that all-important question: What's in it for us if we do change? In the chart at right, check the benefits that you think apply to your organization.

Common Benefits of Teams			
For Organizations	**For Unions**	**For You**	**For Employees**
☐ More efficient operations; reduced cycle time.	☐ More business as a result of becoming more efficient.	☐ A chance to do more value-added things, such as developing and coaching employees.	☐ Increased opportunity to learn jobs across functions (more skill and variety).
☐ More business as a result of becoming more efficient.	☐ More job security for bargaining unit.	☐ Opportunities to manage projects across teams or with customers and suppliers.	☐ Compensation based on pay for skills or team performance.
☐ Improved quality.	☐ More of a say in managing the business.		☐ Opportunities to work more often with customers and suppliers.
☐ Improved customer satisfaction.	☐ More skills training for employees.	☐ More of a say in how the business functions in your area operate.	
☐ Employees taking more responsibility for and ownership of the business.			☐ More skills training.
			☐ More of a say in the business (more decision-making latitude).

What's in It for Employees?

How would you explain to your employees the benefits you checked? Use the spaces provided to jot down some notes on what you would say.

Benefits for our organization:

Benefits for unions:

Benefits for you:

Benefits for employees:

What to Expect Next

Your employees will feel more comfortable with change when you've shared with them what you know about the team implementation and the plan for carrying it out. Use the information you got when you checked with your manager and the steering committee or design team to outline a team implementation plan. Your plan does not have to be complicated; a complete plan should contain these headings:

- A step-by-step process for moving to teams.

- When each step will start and end.

- Who you need to involve to complete each step successfully.

Notes. . .

Month 2

When to Call for Help

- You're having difficulty getting the business data you need to create the case for change. You can call on your manager, the finance department, shipping (for on-time delivery data), and the steering committee or design team.

- Your employees fail to see any benefits of working in teams. Refer to elements of their work that you know appeal to them and show how their jobs would be enhanced by the team implementation.

If You Do Nothing Else . . .

1. Scout around before conducting your all-employee meetings. Find out what would really motivate employees to work with you on the change. Ask at least four employees to get other employees' involvement and test your assumptions.

2. Write down any insights ("aha's!") you had in creating the case for change. If something struck you as interesting, informative, or helpful, it's likely that it will have the same impact on others.

3. Give your employees all the details you have—good or bad. Protecting employees from certain information is sure to give the impression of secrecy and mistrust.

Month at a Glance

MONDAY	TUESDAY	WEDNESDAY	THURSDAY	FRIDAY	SATURDAY/SUNDAY
Check on the status of my request to visit a team organization	Meet with my manager —1½ hours		Read more of the book on empowered teams —1 hour		
		Conduct a "stay-tuned" meeting —1½ hours			
	Prepare basic business information to create motivation for change —1 hour				
			Ask around: What's in it for my employees? —1 hour		

Time Budget

	Goal	Actual
Team coaching	10%	
Project work	10%	
Administrative	70%	
Personal development	10%	

Key Lessons

_____

_____

_____

_____

_____

_____

Next Steps

_____

_____

_____

_____

_____

_____

Preteam Month 3

Notes. . .

Month 3

What to Expect

Many people, once they know about self-directed teams and their benefits, will be eager to start forming teams right away. You should support and encourage this enthusiasm, but you also need to remind everyone that careful planning comes before implementation. While the design team is responsible for planning the overall implementation, you too can play a major role in planning. Following are just some of the topics you and the design team need to consider in order to plan an implementation:

- Who will be on what team. (Team members do not have to come from current groups within the department.)

- New and more proactive roles.

- Skills training at all levels.

- Systems modification.

- Possible equipment moves.

- New measurement methods.

Changes in the Comfort Zone

Redesign or reengineering efforts often require that people (and equipment) move into new work areas and configurations. These moves ensure that employees who work on the same product, group of products, or customers are located together. Such collocation promotes increased communication and cooperation among team members, which can lead to greater productivity, cycle time reductions, and improved quality.

No matter how much people at all levels are involved in planning or implementing the move to teams, some people (including managers) will resist moving out of familiar surroundings. When there is opposition or resistance to change, your job is to try to get everyone to focus on the vision and its objectives. You can do that by asking questions such as:

- "Will we be able to meet the company's objective if we stay the way we are now?"

- "If we don't move now, aren't we likely to move in the future anyway?"

Time to Think and Prepare

Now is the time to think about your role and how it will change; that is, what tasks or responsibilities you will hand off to the team (and how you will do that) and how you will expand your role as coach, consultant, or technical adviser. As with an athlete, you will need to prepare yourself mentally and emotionally for this new role. As you complete this month's activities, consider how doing the following will help you grow into your new role:

- Assess your strengths and developmental areas. How do you stack up to the profile of an empowering leader?

- Check your personal beliefs and actions.

- Develop a training plan for yourself.

- Examine how you spend your time.

Possible Concerns

I've heard that my role will change. I'm okay with that, as long as it doesn't have to happen overnight. How soon will I be expected to be fully up to speed in my new role?

Your employees might expect that you'll share responsibilities with them before teams are formed. This can be a tough transition period for you. Realistically, you can't be expected to change your behavior overnight, but you can get started right away. You will be surprised how much progress you can make in three to four months.

How can I be sure management will support me in my new role? I'm not so sure I want to stick my neck out and risk the consequences.

Ask yourself, If management is asking me to coach employees and I can't or won't, what will happen to me? The answer is pretty obvious. Therefore, you should ask now for the resources you need to be successful. If you receive these resources at the beginning, you can be more certain that management will support you as your role changes.

Your Focus This Month

As you work through this month, focus your efforts on:

- Communicating the case for change.

- How teams and organizations can be redesigned to get results.

- Planning team boundaries.

- How your role will be different in the future.

Week 1
Communicating the case for change

Getting the Message Out

You've gathered a lot of information. Now is the time to communicate it in a way that motivates others.

A meeting of all your employees offers you the best format for presenting this kind of information. There are many factors that will make a meeting succeed or fail. But using the following three tactics will help you ensure that your meetings are informative and productive:

- Face-to-face discussion with questions and answers.

  A guest speaker can dramatically boost the impact of a face-to-face discussion. Ask a knowledgeable person to make a presentation to the team on one aspect of the move to teams. Guest speakers might include:

  — A steering committee member who can talk about the vision and the reasons for the move to teams.

  — A design team member who can answer questions about the implementation plan, design process, site visits, etc.

  — A team member from a part of the organization that has converted to teams. This person can talk about the impact the move to teams has on employees.

  — A union leader involved in the change who could explain the union's support of the change.

- Written information for reading and reference.

- Easily understandable graphics or diagrams.

Planning the Meeting

Let employees know what to expect. Give them a copy of the agenda **before** the meeting.

Sample Agenda

This sample agenda was created for the kind of meeting you'll conduct.

Conference Room 3

8:30   Purpose: to discuss the organization's move to teams and how we will be involved.

8:45   Current status of our business.

9:00   Where we are now and where we need to be.
How teams will get us there: the vision for teams.

9:45   What's in it for us.

10:15 What to expect next: the implementation plan.

10:30 Questions/Next steps.

Making the Meeting Come Alive

Prepare materials that will help you explain the key points in your agenda. Those materials can be flip charts, graphs, diagrams, or any other visual device that excites interest. For example:

1. Create a flip chart that shows the current status of your business.

Sample flip chart

> - *We exceeded our production goals company-wide last year by 5 percent.*
>
> - *We have two new competitors this year.*
>
> - *We lost two contracts to our internal competitor, the Blacksburg facility—they can make it cheaper.*

2. Distribute a graph showing where the organization is now and where it wants to be in the future. Use commonly understood business indicators.

Sample graph

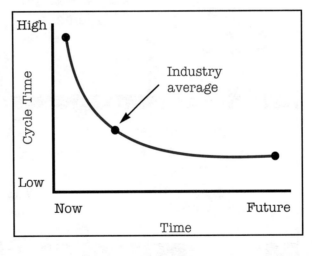

3. On a flip chart list answers to the question, What's in it for us? Ask your employees to add to the list in a brainstorming discussion.

Sample flip chart

> *What's in it for us?*
>
> - *More business = greater job security*
>
> - *More cross-training = fewer headaches in scheduling and more value to organization*

Week 2
Redesigning for results

Reconfiguring Your Work Flow

Your organization might be reorganizing how it produces a product or provides a service. This reengineering or redesign requires that the traditional work-flow boundaries—the handoffs, approvals, regulations, steps, etc.—need to be questioned and possibly replaced with a more seamless, boundaryless system. Not all organizations with self-directed teams redesign their work flow. However, redesign and reengineering produce dramatic results, as mentioned in Preteam Month 1, Week 2.

"Work flow" describes how your work gets done, from start to finish. In many organizations what should be a smooth system is actually a complicated, tradition-bound, stop-and-go process. For instance, the schematic at right (Before Redesign) illustrates the work flow for a company that relied on a highly functionalized work process. The After Redesign diagram on page 33 illustrates how the same product is created when business teams form the core of the organization.

Before Redesign—Work Flow

Tom (an engineer): "I'm planning tests I think are correct." **1**

Delays: Wait on equipment **7a**

Tim (a technician): "I need to wait for directions from engineers." **7**

Traditional supervisor's office: "How can I prioritize all this work?" **3**

Rich (a technician in the test area): "Why do we run these tests anyway?" **4**

Scheduling problems: Conflict in priorities here **6**

Susan (an engineer): "I'm the expert here." **2**

Bob (a technician): "I mix the product and hand it to Rich." **5**

Ken (an engineer): "How am I going to get all my projects done?" **5a**

After Redesign—Organized by Business Teams

Molding Business Team

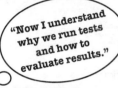

"Now I understand why we run tests and how to evaluate results."

"My work gets done on time."

"Scheduling is no longer a hassle!"

Engineers & Technicians

- Define project scope
- Share expertise daily
- Collocate offices

Empowering supervisors reach consensus on:

- Schedule
- Resources
- Priorities

Results: Cycle time from 3 months to 3 days

Continued on next page ➤

Improving Your Work Flow

The first step to improving how your organization operates is to draw your current work flow process. The diagrams on pages 32 and 33 are examples of what your work flow might look like. Include all the steps, handoffs, reviews, approvals, and physical barriers. Once you've drawn the current work flow, you then can think about ways to improve it. A redesigned process means:

- Better results.

- Employees will have more, and varied, skills.

- Faster cycle time.

- Patients (in a hospital setting) will have shorter waiting periods.

Your current work flow

Typical problems in your work flow:

Handoffs:

Bottlenecks:

Revisions:

Approvals:

Physical barriers:

Improvement Hints

Answering the following questions will help you redesign your work flow in a way that leads to improvements in cycle time, error rate, employee involvement and satisfaction, and productivity.

- Where do most of the problems or errors start in your work flow? (Frequent errors in the process are a good indicator that a redesign is needed.)

- Which of these problems are handed from department to department?

- Where is "wait time" in the process?

- Where and why do things need to be sent back or scrapped?

- Errors (redundant work, increases in your cycle time, and delays) passed from one department to another are often the most costly. How can you better control these errors within the area?

Week 3 (pages 36 and 37) features ideas on how you can help your area control errors before they are passed on to the next unit or to the customer. Make sure you involve others as you think of work flow improvement ideas.

Week 3
Do-it-yourself redesign

Even if your organization has a design team working on overall team architecture, many of the details of what actually gets done in your area will be left up to you and your teams.

Following are some tried-and-true redesign ideas to apply to your own area. Involve the teams in redefining their boundaries and creating new working relationships within the group and with other teams and units throughout the organization. Do not take short cuts here. Well-designed team boundaries will add to your and your teams' success later.

Team Boundary Help File

1. Simplify, simplify, simplify.

    Help the employees find ways to reduce bureaucratic logjams, check points, rules, and signatures that the current system now requires. Remember, the new system should encourage team members to assume more responsibility, adapt to customer needs, and increase their flexibility. Following are some ideas on how to keep team formation from getting complicated:

    • Move equipment to simplify work flow.

    • Have teams facilitate their own meetings.

    • Set up basic guidelines for new responsibilities.

    • Remove physical barriers that hamper communication (for instance, provide a team phone line).

    • Make sure team members have primary membership in one team only.

    • Have employees conduct their own quality inspections.

2. Create close, interdependent associations.

    Reinforce the interdependence that exists between your new teams and people who play pivotal roles in your teams' operations and success. Consider inviting as team members or adjunct team members those key people who interact with your department regularly. As team members, these people could attend team meetings, work on the same goals, attend training with you, and join you in solving problems. As adjunct team members, they could meet with your team monthly. In either case these key people can provide your teams with the information they need to function, while helping the team control errors.

    Maximize interdependence by:

    • Asking key people (for example, purchasing staff, lab technicians, maintenance workers, admitting personnel, shippers, etc.) who work with your team members to join the teams.

    • Solidifing your teams' associations with key people in the organization by setting up formal "points of contact" with team members through regularly scheduled meetings.

3. Control errors within the team.

Teams that can fix or prevent errors will have the greatest chance of succeeding in the new environment. But, for many people, finding and fixing errors was always somebody else's job. Many people will have to make a big shift in attitude if they are going to contribute to their team's error solution efforts. There are four things you can do to help your teams find and fix errors:

- Give the teams the information they need to make decisions on their own.

  For instance, give the team a profit-and-loss statement or a statement of the team's direct and indirect costs, and arrange for them to meet with customers to hear their requirements first hand.

- Update, add, or change technology.

  For instance, make sure the team has access to computers and up-to-date software. Or help them get a bar-scanning system to help teams control their inventory.

- Give the teams authority to change tasks and processes.

  For instance, give the team responsibility for quality checks, ordering and handling materials, and dealing with customer complaints or inaccurate orders.

- Include people from other areas on the team.

4. Cross-train and rotate.

Cross-train team members and rotate them through most of (if not all) the jobs performed by the team. Exposure to all facets of a team's responsibilities raises team members' awareness of each person's impact on processes and quality.

You can promote cross-training by:

- Providing time for all members to learn the process (how all the functions in your area are linked).

- Having the team develop its own cross-training goals. (See pages 100-103 for more ideas.)

Week 4
Changing your role's focus: From microscope to telescope

The last two weeks focused on redesigning or reengineering your group's work flow. That redesign will have a major impact on your employees' work, and on your role, too. Currently, you probably spend the bulk of your time handling crises ("putting out fires"), filling out forms, and dealing with tactical, day-to-day decisions. There's very little time for developing people, planning, training yourself, and other sorts of strategic activities.

In the new team structure you can expect your role to change dramatically. You should find yourself turning over many—if not all—of your tactical responsibilities to the teams. Meanwhile, you will take on a more strategic role, which means you will be coaching team members, handling communications with other teams or groups within the organization, and working on special projects, such as improving customer relations.

In short, your focus will change from the little picture to the big picture: You'll begin to view your work through a telescope instead of a microscope.

How Does My Role Change?

In a team implementation, everyone's roles—what they do on the job to contribute to the organization's vision—will change. Change will come as you, your employees, and your manager adjust to the new realities of the team environment.

You should start thinking now about how to redefine everyone's roles. One way you can do that at this stage in the process is to plot tentative roles and responsibilities for every job layer in your area. Start with the employees; sketch out what you believe they, as new team members, will be doing in the new structure. Then note what activities and functions you and your manager will assume. Be as specific as you can. The illustration shows how responsibilities in a telecommunications center moved from one area to another.

Manager

Expanded Responsibilities
- Teach business awareness
- Create a five-year plan to increase customer and employee satisfaction
- Bring in new business
- Train customers

Keep
- External bid preparation
- Budget review

Supervisor

Expanded Responsibilities
- Vendor evaluation
- Monday update meetings
- New hires
- Customer satisfaction survey coordination

Keep
- Bill payment
- Personnel issues
- Customer issues the team can't handle

Team Members

Expanded Responsibilities
- Resolve problems with customers directly
- Schedule vacations
- Take action to improve team morale
- Train other team members
- Evaluate progress on team goals

Eliminate
- Redundant work procedures
- Double counting on paperwork
- Dead time between jobs

Notes. . .

Month 3

When to Call for Help

- Managers procrastinate on deciding what parts of their role to hand off. Let your design team or steering committee know about this so they can show managers what's in it for them (and you) when they hand responsibility to you.

- You want to improve your team boundaries based on the information in the help file but your manager is reluctant to proceed. Show your manager how the change will reduce cycle time or improve accuracy.

If You Do Nothing Else . . .

1. Make sure you clearly understand what's expected of you when you take on responsibilities once held by your manager. Ask these questions: When will I assume these responsibilities? How will I be evaluated on these responsibilities?

2. Let employees know when they will receive more detailed information regarding team formation and roles.

3. Analyze your work flow now before you unknowingly build barriers into your team formation.

Month at a Glance

MONDAY	TUESDAY	WEDNESDAY	THURSDAY	FRIDAY	SATURDAY/ SUNDAY
Invite a guest speaker —15 minutes		Prepare employee meeting agenda —15 minutes		Prepare employee meeting flip charts —30 minutes	
Conduct the employee meeting —2 hours		Ask for feedback on the employee meeting —1 hour			
	Analyze our current work flow and isolate potential problems —1 hour			Ask employees about work-flow problems —1 hour	
	Consider how my role will change— make a list of how I spend my time —1 hour				

Time Budget

	Goal	Actual
Team coaching	10%	
Project work	10%	
Administrative	70%	
Personal development	10%	

Key Lessons

_____
_____
_____
_____
_____
_____

Next Steps

_____
_____
_____
_____
_____
_____

41

Preteam Month 4

Notes. . .

What to Expect

By now you should be more at ease with the idea of moving to teams. Your new role is taking shape, or at least, you and your manager are talking about what your role will be. You have a better idea of where you're going on the job and what it takes to get you started on the right path. But there's more you must do to make that switch from supervisor to leader.

Your employees also have a long way to go. Yes, they better understand how their roles will change in the developing team setup. And they have a better sense of what's expected of members of a high-performance team. But that doesn't make them a "team." It only makes them more aware of how far they must go to become a fully empowered high-performance team. You and your employees know that if they are to make the move successfully, they will need to start improving and refining their teamwork skills.

This month you can expect to start answering these important questions: How prepared am I, and how prepared are my employees?

Possible Concerns

I just heard that my employees are going to have to go through 52 hours of training in the next nine months. How am I supposed to maintain our service delivery levels with that kind of training schedule?

Many companies use a "time budget" to manage training, allotting about 15 percent of an employee's time to team training activities. That might seem like a lot of time, but there are ways to manage training time to everyone's advantage. Consider doing some of the following:

- Conduct training during downtime.

- Use employees from other areas to fill in temporarily.

- Work overtime as teams ramp up.

- Remove non-value-added, unnecessary process steps (such as rework, multiple reviews, redundant sampling, etc.).

Yeah, but what if my manager won't change?

Another way to phrase this concern is, How can I empower employees to do things I am not empowered to do myself? It's true, your manager needs to empower you so you can empower others. If your manager doesn't do that, however, you have one usually persuasive course of action: Meet with your manager often and demonstrate that you and your employees are capable of handling more responsibility. Don't take the easy way out and think, My manager is not empowering, so I don't have to be.

Will I be held responsible for mistakes the teams make?

A plant manager once said, "Employees don't make mistakes on purpose. They make mistakes when their managers neglect to give them the information and support they need to do their jobs correctly." You will be responsible for guiding and developing your employees to run their operation or service as if it were their own business. Expect that people will make mistakes; that's a natural part of the learning process. However, with your help teams will not make mistakes that jeopardize the business.

Your Focus This Month

During the next four weeks you will focus your efforts on:

- Preparing for your new role as a leader.

- Deciding how you can spend your time more wisely.

- Developing a baseline against which to measure progress.

- Building your employees' skills as future team members.

Week 1
Preparing for your new role

Now vs. the Future

Last month you looked at how roles would be changing in the move to teams. Most leaders find that their roles change significantly. Complete the following activities to develop a more specific plan for your role change.

1. Refer to your calendar, production reports, or minutes of meetings. List all the tasks you've worked on during the last two months, including the less-than-glamorous tasks:

2. Some tasks don't add value to your product or service. Following are examples non-value-added activities, some of which might apply to your job. Review the tasks you listed in item 1. Check those tasks that do not add value to your product, service, or business. Do you:

    *   Review other people's work? (Such as, review an operator's batch report nightly.)

    *   Move materials or people back and forth? (Such as, run patients to and from radiology.)

    *   Do a lot of rework? (Such as, rewrite an employee's report without adding significant value.)

    *   Sign paperwork that employees have already completed and checked? (Such as, audit reports, production logs.)

3. Refer to the Empowerment Schedule (page 11). Highlight any tasks that match those you listed in item 1 on page 44. These are the tasks you need to coach teams on during the next 6 to12 months. Eventually, your teams will be responsible for these tasks. List those that you need to coach the teams to handle here:

4. Take a look at how your role might expand during the next two years. In the left column list your manager's tasks, then check those you can take on as your employees assume more of your responsibilities. In the right column list those tasks you need to prepare for as part of a career path option. An example is provided in italics.

My Manager's Task List	Career Option Tasks
Write the budget for the area's six line items for next year.	*Facilitate the obstetrics unit's move to teams next month to build my team skills.*

Week 2

Time management for team leaders

Teams require a whole new focus. Successful leaders of teams find that their work days change dramatically. To gauge how teams will affect your days, refer to your current list of tasks (page 44). Classify the tasks into one of four categories listed below, then estimate how much time (as a percent of total) you spend each day in each category. (The pie chart illustrates business average.)

Your Current Role

_____% Administrative paperwork and telephone calls

_____% Personal development

_____% Developing others (coaching, training, etc.)

_____% Special projects

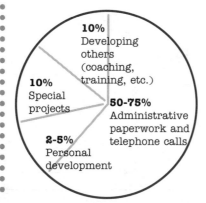

Your New Role

As your organization moves to teams, you will pass on some responsibilities to your employees, and take on some of your manager's tasks. Using the same categories as above, estimate how you would like to spend your time in your new role. (The pie chart illustrates business average.)

_____% Administrative paperwork and telephone calls

_____% Personal development

_____% Developing others (coaching, training, etc.)

_____% Special projects

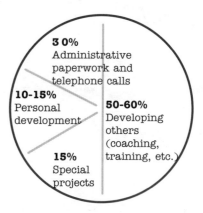

What You Can Do

You've already thought about eliminating non-value-added tasks from your current role. What else can you do to move toward your new role? Following are examples of what you can do:

- Spend at least 50 percent more time on developing your skills in interacting with other people.

- Stay focused on your training commitments.

- Review your calendar each month and check how you spend your time. Are you under target on the amount of time you spend coaching? Is too little time devoted to personal development? If you can answer yes to either question, what can you do to reorder your priorities?

Add to them now, or complete the list later as you become more familiar with what you want to achieve and how you can go about achieving it.

What else can I do?

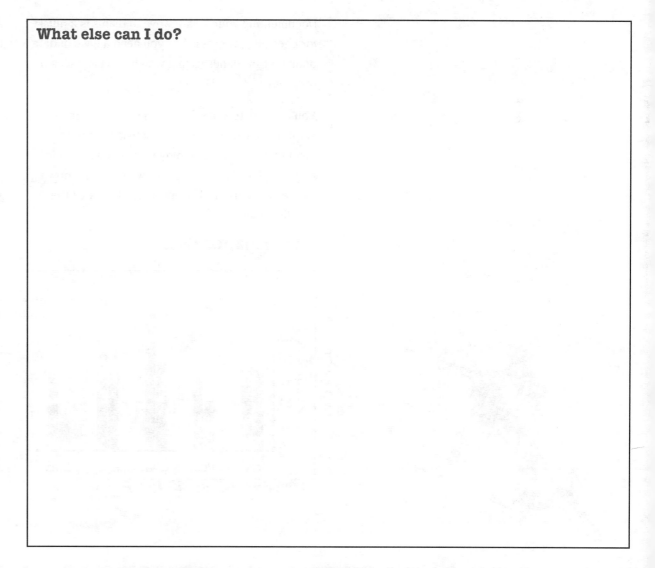

Week 3
How to assess progress

Documenting your area's move to teams is a must for checking progress. But you need a base of data points, or baseline, against which you can measure progress.

You can create a baseline by measuring your employees' performance and satisfaction now, before you and your employees begin working in teams. A baseline is simply a "watermark" showing where you started. This example illustrates the baseline concept:

Performance Baseline

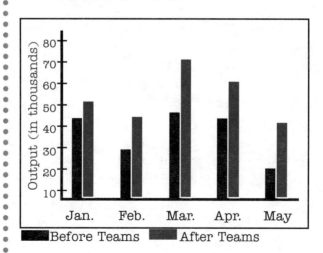

After your teams are up and running, you can use the data you uncover in creating a baseline to:

- Detect if teams are off track.

- Show top management bottom-line progress.

- Celebrate team progress.

Creating a Baseline

The best, most informative baselines use data collected over several months and on a number of different indicators. You can use data from production reports, employee opinion surveys, error rate reports, and similar tracking techniques to create a baseline chart similar to the one on page 49. You should gather data for at least three or four months before the team start-up.

Team start-up

Sample Baseline

Measure	J	F	M	A	M	J	J	A	S	O	N	D
Rework (%)	30%	32%	28%	25%	23%	23%	22%					
Degree of Empowerment	2	2	3	3	3	3	4					
% On-time Delivery	75	80	85	83	75	80	80					
% Accurate Shipments	80	75	75	77	72	75	80					

Refer to the example to create your own baseline. Use this form. How can you get your teams to complete the baseline?

Measure	J	F	M	A	M	J	J	A	S	O	N	D

Week 4
Building your employees' skills

Team start-ups go more smoothly when the employees who will be affected by the move know something about teams and teamwork. You will spend less time explaining teams and teamwork if employees are given the basics early on. Following are four areas of basic team training and key learning points for each area. Place a check mark by each key learning point that you think could benefit your employees.

1. How to be an empowered associate

☐ The responsibility for empowerment has to be shared by leaders and employees. Employees' responsibility is to accept changes that go along with gaining new skills.

☐ Key elements of an effective, empowered employee.

2. What are high-performance teams?

☐ Differences between high-performance teams and "teamwork."

☐ How these types of teams evolve over time.

☐ How the leader actually shares responsibilities over time.

☐ Examples of how these teams have been successful in other companies.

3. What to expect as you work in teams

☐ Factors that separate high-performance teams from average teams or low-performance teams.

☐ Stages that teams go through as they develop, and how to progress from one stage to the next.

4. Valuing differences

☐ How differences in employees' styles and preferences can be used to the team's advantage.

☐ What employees' styles or preferences are so they better understand themselves and how they can contribute to the team.

Reinforcing on-the-job Training

Training will be a waste of time and money if the employees don't get a chance to use what they've learned on the job. As a leader you play a valuable role in making sure employees can transfer new skills to the job. Your reinforcement of their training tells employees that you value what they've learned and want to help them succeed.

You can do several things to show employees that you value training:

- Attend the same training programs your employees attend.

- Discuss the training at a staff meeting.

- Ask employees how they can apply the new skills and concepts on the job.

- Praise employees who apply new skills to their work.

- Discuss your expectations about empowered associates, valuing differences, or working in teams.

Describe three things you can do to support your employees' training. Write your ideas below. Use your calendar to remind yourself to do this periodically.

1.

2.

3.

Notes. . .

M o n t h   4

When to Call for Help

- If employees don't seem to understand the training they attended. Discuss the issue with the trainer, who might be able to explain why the training didn't "take" or modify the training to make it more useful.

- Some supervisors won't cooperate with you in your employee training efforts. Others might even minimize what you're doing. If your attempts to win these people over has failed, mention it to your manager. Suggest a meeting of all supervisors at which your manager can reinforce how everyone's support is needed for the move to teams.

- You and your manager can't agree on clearly defined roles and responsibilities. Your manager might not know everything about the move to teams; ask members of the design team or steering committee for more information about how roles should be changing. Discuss this information with your manager until you both understand roles, objectives, and measures of success.

If You Do Nothing Else . . .

1. See that your employees enroll in skill-building training. Don't shortcut training.

2. Show that you are committed to the team effort: Give your employees a task you normally do. Delegating power in this way will start you on the road to establishing a true partnership with your employees.

3. Show that you value the training your employees are getting by attending their training sessions.

Month at a Glance

MONDAY	TUESDAY	WEDNESDAY	THURSDAY	FRIDAY	SATURDAY/ SUNDAY
	Redesign my role—eliminate non-value-added tasks, set coaching priorities —2 hours				
	Determine how I spend my time now —1¹⁄₂ hours		Review my role changes with my manager —1 hour		
	Develop a baseline —2 hours		Ask employees for ideas on the baseline —1 hour	Explain importance of next week's skills training —30 minutes	
	Attend employee skills training —2 hours		Discuss the baseline in an employee meeting —1 hour	Reinforce employees' use of new skills on the job —30 minutes	

Time Budget

	Goal	Actual
Team coaching	10%	
Project work	10%	
Administrative	70%	
Personal development	10%	

Key Lessons

_____

_____

_____

_____

_____

_____

Next Steps

_____

_____

_____

_____

_____

_____

Preteam Month 5

Notes. . .

Month 5

What to Expect

As a frontline leader, you have more influence on how employees react to and work with change than just about anyone else. For that reason alone you are valuable to the organization's future. Therefore, it's important for you not to under-estimate how your opinions and actions influence employees, who have looked up to you for years. The activities you must stress with your employees this month include improving everyone's skills and responsibilities so your organization can remain competitive.

Possible Concerns

What if I slide back to my old behaviors early in the move to teams?

Early on, setbacks are not unusual. You can handle a setback by:

- Admitting that you made a mistake or that you temporarily slid into your old role.

- Discussing with the people involved what happened that led you to fall back into your "supervisor" role. Be willing to talk openly with people; generally, they will be sympathetic to the difficulties you face as you make the transition to leader.

- Finding out what made a situation stressful. People often revert to the old way of doing things when they are under pressure or when trying to deal with an emergency. Eliminating the causes of stress is one way to avoid slipping into old styles of behavior.

Teams look great on paper. How do I make it happen in reality?

As you start the New Team Phase, the survival guide will suggest meetings you can conduct to help your employees pull together as a team. Make sure you work with your employees to develop a team charter and a business plan with goals. Take one step at a time, do not skip steps, and your teams will start off on the right foot.

Your Focus This Month

As you proceed on your voyage to teams, this month you will focus on:

- Continuing to build your employees' skills.

- Sharing authority with your employees.

- Continuing to build your own skills.

- Finalizing your role with your manager.

Week 1

Increasing employee horsepower: Building skills—continued

Your employees might be charged up after their initial awareness training and eager to enhance their skills. The skills described below will help you fuel the momentum for teams within your employees. Review the skills and learning points below. Check the skills that are training priorities for your employees.

1. **Participating in Meetings**

   ☐ Prepare and follow effective agendas.

   ☐ Get meetings back on track.

   ☐ Balance participation.

2. **Communicating with Others**

   ☐ Practice reducing communication barriers by:

   • Maintaining self-esteem.

   • Listening and responding with empathy.

   • Asking for help.

   ☐ Learn how to give feedback that maintains self-esteem, and receive feedback without becoming resentful or defensive.

   ☐ Meet other people's personal needs to be heard and listened to.

3. **Providing First-rate Service**

   ☐ Take the heat from angry customers (internal and external).

   ☐ Understand the importance of good service to customers, the organization, and you.

   ☐ Better understand customers' needs.

   ☐ Recognize that customer contact people make the difference in meeting customer expectations.

4. **Reaching Agreement as a Team**

   ☐ Involve others to build their commitment to an objective, idea, project, or new venture.

   ☐ Build consensus in the group; total agreement isn't always necessary.

   ☐ Learn how to reduce options, discuss them, and select an acceptable option.

Transferring Skills

As a leader you play an important role in ensuring that skills learned in training are transferred to the job. One way you can do this is to reinforce your employees whenever they use a new skill. Following are some ways to show that you support your employees' training efforts and that you want to reinforce them.

- Always use an agenda for staff meetings that includes tasks and time frames. At the end of each meeting develop the next meeting's agenda.

- Make suggestions to get staff meetings back on track.

- When members are silent or do not participate, try to draw them into the discussion by asking them directly for their ideas.

- In every interaction with an employee, maintain or enhance that person's self-esteem.

- Model how to provide service to customers.

Skills Reinforcement Contract

Complete this "contract." It will put you on record as stating your intentions to help your employees grow in their new roles.

I agree to do the following to reinforce employees' skills:

1.

2.

3.

4.

Week 2

No guts, no glory: Sharing your leadership responsibility

Delegating some of your tasks—sharing leadership responsibility—is a good way to start building a high level of trust between you and your employees. It also builds your confidence as you move into your new role. When sharing responsibility it's important to ensure that you make a win-win situation for everyone: Select a task that is easily handled and then assign it to someone you believe can do it successfully. Follow these steps to ensure that your early efforts succeed:

1. Assess your employees' readiness for taking on a new task. If your group is in the middle of major changes, wait until the work load and pace have stabilized. Consider transferring responsibilities that:

- Will excite employees.

- Will have enough impact that employees will take you seriously.

- Are a natural progression from tasks the employees do now.

2. Decide which task you want to start with. Write your ideas below. Examples of tasks you can delegate are included.

Task to delegate   **To whom?**

- *Tracking performance*

- *Filling out work orders*

- *Calling maintenance directly*

- *Scheduling*

- *Getting materials directly*

3. Explain the task thoroughly and describe what it takes to successfully complete it. Include:

- Critical parts of the task.

- How the task affects other people or departments.

- The expected outcomes and how long it will probably take to complete the task.

- Major obstacles that employees might encounter.

4. Encourage your employees to assume the task as part of their jobs. Ask questions that will start them thinking about how to accomplish the task. Write your questions below for one task; sample questions are included.

Task:

Sample Questions:

- *What would your follow-up steps be?*

- *What would you do if you couldn't complete the task on time?*

- *How would you get others involved in the task?*

Other Questions:

How Did It Go?

You can tell it went well if:

- You did not jump in and take over.

- You let the employee decide how to accomplish the task, even if you would have done it differently.

- You avoided over-explaining the task.

- You asked open-ended questions and did not tell the employee what to do.

- You were able to do something else instead of working on that task.

- The task was done properly and without direct supervision from you.

Answer these questions to assess your first attempt at transferring responsibility:

1. What did I do well that I want to repeat?   **2. What will I do differently the next time I give authority?**

Week 3

Increasing your own horsepower: Leadership skills

You've completed your reading and awareness building about teams and leaders of teams. Now it's time to hone your skills in preparation for leading teams. Review the key learning points for each of the following six skill areas and check those you want to include in your training. Note some ideas on how you can use each learning point with your teams.

1. Building Trust

☐ Understand how what you are doing builds (or destroys) successful relationships.

☐ Recognize patterns of mistrust and how they damage productivity, quality, and morale.

☐ Know how to avoid common trust traps (making assumptions, covering yourself, breaking promises, shooting the messenger, mixing messages, and sugarcoating).

What I can do to build trust with my employees:

2. Encouraging Initiative

☐ Avoid judging ideas until all the information is presented.

☐ Trust people to use their ideas in challenging ways and be willing to take risks.

What I can do to encourage initiative among my employees:

3. Coaching

☐ Guide others to think for themselves.

☐ Balance telling and seeking to encourage involvement and ownership of the task.

☐ Develop all team members into high performers.

What I can do to coach my employees:

4. Giving and Receiving Feedback

☐ Give feedback that energizes employees to improve.

☐ Receive feedback without getting defensive.

☐ Practice handling difficult feedback sessions.

What I can do to promote the giving and receiving of feedback:

6. Leading Effective Meetings

☐ Prepare and follow agenda.

☐ Make suggestions to keep meetings on track.

☐ Follow guidelines to ensure that agenda items are discussed, summarized, and developed into action items.

What I can do to lead more effective meetings:

An Ideal Opportunity

5. Overcoming Resistance to Change

☐ Provide information about the change and how the change will affect people.

☐ Anticipate concerns before they become larger issues.

☐ Involve people in the process by asking for their input.

What I can do to help my employees overcome resistance to change:

While you're at training your employees have a chance to make day-to-day decisions. Think about what you can pass along to your employees and write your ideas below. Answer this question: What can employees take on (what decisions can they make) while I'm at training?

What	Who	Help I Need to Provide

Week 4
Checkpoint #2: Finalizing your role with your manager

Solidifying your new role with your manager is a critical step for you—and your employees. If you skip this opportunity, you can't be sure your manager will support your team development plans or give you the credit you deserve for coaching your employees.

Schedule a meeting with your manager to review the issues and topics listed at right. Try to pin down specific outcomes for each topic. Use the space provided for taking notes or listing agreed-upon outcomes. At the end of the meeting, you and your manager should have a clear picture of your new responsibilities, training needs, measurement methods, and more.

☐ List of duties you will hand off, keep, and expand.

☐ Percent of time to be spent on coaching, personal development, special projects, etc.

☐ My training plan.

☐ Schedule for receiving feedback on my performance in the new role. (Suggested schedule: at least once every three months.)

☐ Specific goals for my new role and how my manager will measure success. Refer to the responsibility tracking form on page 63 for ideas on what to track and how to document it. Review the example for ideas on how to create your own form.

Sample Role Agreement

Responsibility	Goals	Measures	Feedback Date
Coaching	• *Spend 50 percent of time developing employee technical skills and team collaboration.* • *Team members learn one new skill every 6 months.* • *80 percent of team members satisfied with coaching.* • *Teams take on at least 80 percent of the tasks at 3-month point on Empowerment Schedule.*	• *Month-end checks on how I spend my time.* • *Progress on team cross-training plan.* • *Team satisfaction survey.* • *Empowerment Schedule check.*	

☐ Resources I need from my manager during the next three months. For example:

- Temporary employees.

- Use of overtime budget.

- Employees from another shift or area to assist in production/service delivery.

- Access to my manager for coaching on tough situations.

- Access to support professionals for face-to-face meetings with employees.

- Cooperation from other supervisors who are not now working in teams.

Use this form or one like it to list the resources you need, when you need them, and who will provide them to you.

Resources My Manager or the Organization Can Provide		
What	By When	From Whom

Notes. . .

Month 5

When to Call for Help

- Other supervisors or leaders might respond negatively to your emphasis on employee training. Consider holding a preview session just for them. The purpose of that session would be to review the materials and skills employees will learn. Make sure you emphasize how good use of these skills will make the supervisors' jobs a little easier.

- If you're still unclear about your new role, spend time getting all the detailed answers you need from other supervisors with teams or from your manager.

If You Do Nothing Else . . .

1. Prepare your employees before they go to training. Explain the training objectives, what you hope they gain from the training, and how they will have their jobs covered.

2. Discuss your training and your new role with all your employees. Make sure they understand how your role is changing.

3. Schedule follow-up meetings to discuss your progress with your manager.

Month at a Glance

MONDAY	TUESDAY	WEDNESDAY	THURSDAY	FRIDAY	SATURDAY/ SUNDAY
	Employee skills training —4 hours	Employee skills training —4 hours			
		Practice giving more leadership responsibility —1 hour		Actual hand-off coaching discussion —1 hour	
	Leader skills training —4 hours		Leader skills training —4 hours	Discuss my training with employees —30 minutes	
Memo to employees regarding skills training part 2	Find backups to fill in for Thursday and Friday —1 hour		Finalize my new role with my manager —2 hours		

Time Budget

	Goal	Actual
Team coaching	10%	
Project work	10%	
Administrative	70%	
Personal development	10%	

Key Lessons

_____

_____

_____

_____

_____

_____

Next Steps

_____

_____

_____

_____

_____

Preteam Month 6

Notes. . .

Month 6

What to Expect

You and most of your employees should feel prepared to launch into teams. Just two short months ago most of you were probably in the dark. But now everyone should have a clearer understanding of what's expected of a team and of them. Your preparation has enabled you to come a long way to reach this point.

Nevertheless, there still may be a few holdouts, some people who continue to be skeptical about the move to teams. Skeptics are easy to identify: They don't participate or ask questions; they rehash questions you thought were answered; and they repeatedly say, "There's nothing new here."

Eventually you should be able to get most skeptics on board. But right now you don't want to devote too much time and energy to doing that. Instead, you should be building enthusiasm with those employees who are trying to help you make the change succeed. The skeptics will come on board when they see that the changes have produced results.

Possible Concerns

I'm not comfortable with employees making decisions about the quality of our product or service. They don't even understand our customers' requirements or how we stack up to our competitors.

Employees who know little about customer requirements or competitive advantages should not be expected to, nor will they be able to, make informed decisions about product or service quality. But you can do something about that by starting to educate them now. Use what you know about customer requirements and the competition.

To formulate a plan for educating your employees, answer questions such as what changes are the competitors making and what changes are we making to meet customer requirements. These are the kinds of questions employees might ask if given the responsibility for making decisions around quality. The answers are a good starting point for educating your employees.

I know we have spent the last few months preparing to work in teams. We have done a lot of things the right way, and I feel good about that. But now I'm worried. What if we don't produce results that are far and above what we can do right now?

The key to producing positive results with empowered work teams is to follow the format of this guide. If you complete the activities and exercises to the best of your ability, you and your teams will be able to produce the kind of results that will make the transition to teams worthwhile and beneficial.

Team implementations fail when key parts of the team model are left out or completed poorly. Key elements that are part of every successful team implementation are:

- Clear, specific vision and values with behaviors that describe how far and how fast the teams are to progress toward empowerment.

- Team boundaries that enable members to control as many of the decisions and problems as possible from start to finish in the core process.

- Specific roles and responsibilities that match the vision at all levels.

- Skills training to equip employees, leaders, and managers to live the values.

- Measurements on team-based production, quality, and employee development that provide feedback to everyone about how well the teams are working.

Your Focus This Month

This month you will be focusing on:

- Dealing with performance problems on the teams.

- Handling skeptics.

- Building a greater level of trust between you and the team members.

- Working with your manager.

Week 1
Dealing with performance problems

Some leaders assume that peer pressure in teams will handle recurring performance problems effectively. While peer pressure can help team performance, don't expect members in new teams to be able to address persistent performance problems. You will do your employees and yourself a favor if you address employee performance problems *now* and if you make it clear that you will continue to handle performance problems for the foreseeable future. Following are examples of real-life performance problems and what the leaders did to rectify them.

Situation 1

When employees working on a rail car repair assembly line finished their assigned work, they would wait until new work arrived at their station. If other stations needed help, they wouldn't offer to pitch in, even though in most cases they had the expertise that was needed.

The leader's response: The leader met with each employee and explained that he knew in the past they were not "allowed" to leave their stations. Now, he said, the goals would require them to back up each other.

To make sure that happened, the leader created a backup position that each employee went to after completing his or her work. The leader followed up by reminding employees to go to their backup station when they completed their work early.

Situation 2

Two patient-focused care teams had problems sharing resources. The emergency room and cardiac rehabilitation team leaders did not collaborate on moving patients from one area to another. Often, when the emergency room leader tried to move patients from the emergency room to the cardiac unit for stabilized care, the cardiac unit leader would report "no beds available" when, in fact, beds were available. The result: Patients were moved from unit to unit and, sometimes, to another hospital.

The leader's response: The hospital administrator called the directors together to meet on the issue. She discussed how this problem cost the hospital more than $30,000 in lost fees and led to patient inconvenience and frustration. She made her expectations clear: Unit leaders would cooperate so that the hospital could operate efficiently.

Situation 3

A field territory slated to convert to self-directed teams had to figure out how to deal with a district sales representative who had a history of poor performance (not returning customers' telephone calls, leaving early on Friday, and so forth).

The leader's response: The zone manager decided to address the problem before the team start-up. He found out that the rep was much better suited to a more structured work situation. He was able to transfer her to a home office job before that territory converted to teams.

What similar difficulties with performance do you have or anticipate having as your area moves to teams?

Guidelines for Solving Performance Problems

Most, if not all, of these problems can be handled in one-on-one conversations with the employee. Try applying the sample guidelines below to your employees' performance problems before the move to teams. Remember, when discussing performance problems you should focus on the **problem**, not the **person.**

1. Describe the problem in a friendly manner. Be specific and sincere and focus on the problem, not the person.

2. Ask for the employee's help in solving the problem. Let the employee take an active part in the solution.

3. Discuss causes for the problem. Ask for the employee's ideas, using open-ended questions. Summarize the causes.

4. Identify and write down possible solutions. Make sure you write the employee's solution first; offer your solution as an alternative if the employee's solution is not workable.

5. Decide on actions each of you should take. Developing a plan that incorporates the employee's ideas reinforces the employee's commitment to change his or her behavior.

6. Agree on a specific date and time for following up on the action plan.

Week 2
Navigating with a skeptical crew

Do you find yourself trying to combat employee skepticism? When an employee reacts skeptically to a change, do you say to yourself, Not this again? Do you attempt to oversell an employee on all the benefits of a change? Most leaders encounter a fair amount of employee skepticism on the way to culture change. (Usually, about 10 percent of employees are hard-core skeptics.) You may be on employee skepticism overload, but these employees need your help. To pinpoint the reasons for the skepticism and how to handle it, complete the following exercise.

1. Listen to your employees' problems with the vision and move to teams. Remember, just because employees complain about taking on more responsibility, that doesn't mean they don't want or won't take on more responsibilities. They might just want to be heard. List your employees' concerns on the left. On the right are some ways you can show that you want to help.

My employees' major issues are:	How I demonstrate that I hear their issues:
	• *Active listening; paraphrasing what was said.*
	• *Respond with empathy, not sympathy.*
	• *Present their concerns to management.*
	• *Solve issues where I can.*
	• *Hear them out, whether or not I agree with them.*

2. What's causing employee resistance? Personal fears you can help with or organizational policies and systems you can help change? Check any of the following that apply to your "resistors."

Personal Fears

☐ Lack of skills to cross-train

☐ Years spent building work procedures

☐ Unaccustomed to new tasks

Organizational Systems or Policies

☐ Praise, recognition for old-school behaviors

☐ Policies dictate what employees can/can't do

☐ Decades of rigid procedure manuals to follow

3. Now you can address the cause and begin to ease employee skepticism. Review these lists of actions and place a check mark by those that you feel comfortable trying.

Actions to address personal fears:

☐ Let employees create a cross-training plan.

☐ Help deliver cross-training.

☐ Make sure those doing the cross-training can train others, not just show off.

☐ Spread changes out over several months to prevent "change overload."

☐ Give your key resistors important responsibilities related to the change, such as leading a discussion or preparing a plan.

☐ Take your resistors on a visit to a company where teams are successful.

☐ Ask skeptics to make a presentation about upcoming changes.

Actions to address organizational systems or policies:

☐ Encourage employees to use their own judgment and expertise to handle issues that don't have or require step-by-step procedures. (Be sure to reinforce safety.)

☐ Change procedures that prevent cross-training or awareness of your work flow from start to finish.

☐ Reinforce employees who try new behaviors.

☐ Involve employees in redesigning constraining procedures.

☐ Ask a manager to come in and reinforce new ways of doing things.

Week 3
Trust must come first

By now you will undoubtedly have more detailed information to discuss with your employees. You will want to talk about that information in a way that strengthens your employees' trust in you and your trust in them.

Trust Reality Check

When you communicate with your employees, how well do you build trust? Your words and responses to questions or challenges send a clear message. Sometimes the message might undercut trust—and you're not even aware that it is happening. Everyone falls into this "trust trap" once in a while. Therefore, it's important that you evaluate your effectiveness at building trust before you communicate important messages to your employees.

Read the following questions and place a check mark by those that describe your style. (You can give your employees copies of the Trust Reality Check to evaluate you.)

Do you find yourself:

☐ Assuming someone is going to refuse a request?

☐ Covering yourself by deflecting blame to someone else?

☐ Economizing trust by not telling the whole story or giving all the information you have?

☐ Forcing decisions or plans that favor you at the expense of others?

☐ Refusing to make commitments that could put you at risk?

☐ Talking behind people's backs?

☐ Breaking confidences?

☐ Not following through on actions you said you would complete or resources you said you would provide?

☐ Shooting the messenger?

☐ Supporting employees one day and leaving them stranded the next?

☐ Hiding problems from employees by talking around the issue or sugarcoating it?

If you checked any of the trust traps, refer to the following ideas for building trust with your employees. Review the items and then list some ideas for what you need to do to create a high level of trust with your employees.

How to Rebuild Trust

- Keep the Trust Reality Check handy and review it before your meetings.

- Ask an employee you trust and respect to confront you when you start falling into a trust trap.

- Follow up to show you've understood.

- Let the other person do most of the talking.

- When appropriate, acknowledge that you don't know all the answers.

- Ask others for feedback and then use their feedback.

- Tell people that you have confidence in their abilities.

What I need to do.	What I can do next week to demonstrate this.

Week 4
Checkpoint #3: Reviewing progress

Team Progress Review Planner

Be sure to update your manager on your progress and your teams' progress. Meet formally with your manager once every three or four months to review progress. Use the suggested format below to prepare yourself. After the meeting evaluate how well it went by answering the questions on page 75.

Agenda	Meeting Preparation Notes
8:00 Major tasks the team has been working on New responsibilities/decisions	Behavior/Attitude changes: Productivity or quality changes:
8:20 External barriers impeding team progress	My ideas for removing these barriers:
8:40 Internal barriers impeding team progress	My ideas for removing these barriers:
9:00 How I have been spending my time What is working well with my new role What has **not** been working well with my role that I would like to improve	My ideas about what I should be doing in the next few months: Your ideas for what I should be doing:

9:15 Resources I need from my manager to improve team functioning:
 	
    • More technical training time
 	
    • Manager spends more time with the team
	How much? By when?

9:30 End of meeting To-do list	Summarize conclusions.

Meeting Evaluation

1. How did you feel when you left the meeting with your manager?

2. What topics would you stress during your next meeting?

3. How did your manager react to your team's progress? Your ideas for overcoming barriers?

4. What will you tell the team as a result of this meeting?

5. Discuss review meetings with other leaders. What did they say or do that was effective and that you could use next time?

When to Call for Help

- You find out that the trust level between you and your employees is worse than you thought. Ask a neutral third party to help you regenerate trust (human resources, the design team, or another leader).

- You can't seem to get the training you need when you need it. Build a case for more training. Enlist the help of fellow leaders and human resources contacts. Sell a proposal for more training to upper management or the steering committee.

- Your employees' performance problems seem unresolvable. Seek advice from your manager or leaders who have successfully handled the kinds of problems you face.

If You Do Nothing Else . . .

1. Address the skeptics' concerns. After all, the organization is changing the rules that set the standard for workplace behavior and productivity. Give your employees a chance to adapt to the new situation.

2. Build trust early, before you are expected to lead teams. Your teams will progress faster if you generate trust and support.

3. Use the skills you practiced in training. Almost everyone can benefit from using the training they learned. Remember, if you don't use them now, you might have difficulty using them later, when you'll need them the most.

Month at a Glance

MONDAY	TUESDAY	WEDNESDAY	THURSDAY	FRIDAY	SATURDAY/SUNDAY
	Identify top two performance problems and plan how to handle them —1 hour		Pass on any news to the employees —1 hour		
Write a plan to address major skeptics' issues —2 hours		Start the plan with the skeptics —1 hour		Follow up on performance problems—how is it going? —1 hour	
	Photocopy the Trust Reality Check and complete it —15 minutes	Ask employees to complete the Trust Reality Check about me —30 minutes		Create a plan to improve trust in my department —1 hour	
Meet with manager —1½ hours Complete debriefing from meeting —30 minutes	Complete Step 1 of my trust plan —1 hour		Follow up with skeptics: How are they doing?	Complete Step 2 of my trust plan —2 hours	

Time Budget

	Goal	Actual
Team coaching	20%	
Project work	10%	
Administrative	60%	
Personal development	10%	

Key Lessons

_____

_____

_____

_____

_____

_____

Next Steps

_____

_____

_____

_____

_____

_____

_____

Notes. . .

New Team Development Phase

You and your employees are now ready to launch into some unfamiliar seas, those of the newly formed teams. Over the next few months you and the members of your teams will be sailing into new opportunities, and up to and around unfamiliar obstacles. Use the activities on the following pages to help steer your teams through the narrows and straits of the first part of the New Team Phase.

Month 1

- Okay, how do we start?
- Productive team meetings
- Creating accountability on your teams
- Clarifying the star points

Month 2

- Selecting team members for star points
- Energizing new teams
- Sharing work in a team
- Building understanding through cross-training

Month 3

- Building your skills—continued
- Creating team business plans
- Taking the teams' temperature—Part 1
- Celebrating success

Month 4

- Sharing more of your old role
- Turbocharged team skills: Building skills—continued
- Eye appeal: Visual progress tracking
- Checkpoint #4: Staying in touch

Month 5

- Are your teams becoming more self-directed?
- Discussing progress on the business plan
- Fostering interdependence
- Providing more challenging decisions

Month 6

- Common barriers and how to bust them
- More on busting barriers
- Did I spend my time wisely?
- Recognizing six months of hard work

New Team Month 1

Notes. . .

What to Expect

This is it! After months of preparation, you've finally set sail. At this important stage in the growth process, you'll be providing your teams with many new tasks and responsibilities—and assistance. New teams need structure to get off to a good start, especially if your organization has a reputation (deserved or not) for not following through on initiatives.

Like you, your employees might be confused at first about their roles, how they interact with other departments or shifts, and how much authority they have. Weeks 1 and 2 for this month will help clarify and resolve these issues. You will find it helpful to continually refer to the charter and roles you will develop this month. Use the charter as your beacon to light your way.

If part of your area is not going to teams (while other parts are), you probably are feeling somewhat schizophrenic! You're working with the new teams in one way and with other areas in the old way. Most leaders who face this challenge get through it by gradually applying some aspects of their new role (training, one-on-one coaching, more involvement in staff meetings) with the more traditional areas.

Possible Concerns

I don't like a lot of structure. I like to just get going. Don't we need to let the teams make decisions and answer some of their own questions about getting started instead of providing structure for them?

During the first few months of the New Team Phase, your teams will be too new and inexperienced to progress on their own. Yes, if they have the right combination of knowledge, skills, and abilities, you should let them make many of their own decisions. But don't underestimate the value of structure: Teams that operate with a structure (charter, decision-making tools, goals, and measures) produce significantly better results than teams that must find their way without the right tools, training, guidance, or support.

I'm concerned about informal leaders emerging in the team. I think two or three of my employees believe that the move to teams is their chance to become "supervisors" to the rest of their team members.

If left unchecked, informal leaders with the wrong idea about their roles can drag your team off track and create internal struggling. Use the team start-up process to address this issue head on.

Your Focus This Month

As you start working with your teams, this month you will focus on:

- Chartering the teams.

- Making team meetings productive.

- Developing accountability for new responsibilities.

- Clarifying shared leadership roles.

Week 1
Okay, how do we start?

Every team needs a charter. A charter clearly and simply states a team's purpose, operating guidelines, responsibilities, measures of success, and scope of authority. Making sure your new teams have a charter is one of the best things you can do to get them started on the path to success.

Team charters have many benefits:

- *A charter focuses the team.* Creating a charter helps a team narrow the scope of its tasks, thus ensuring that everyone works together toward the same objectives.

  Your job: Use charters to align teams within your area and across shifts.

- *A charter helps build the team.* With a charter your employees are more likely to be a team and not just a collection of people working at similar tasks. For many members, completing a charter is one of the first accomplishments they will make as a team. A charter also develops a team's sense of pride.

  Your job: Celebrate completing the charter. Help the team publicize it.

- *A charter reduces conflict.* The operating guidelines the team develops as part of its charter help resolve differences and help prevent long discussions about "the real reason we're here" or "is that our job?" Because the team—and not management—writes the charter, it should go a long way toward eliminating (or at least easing) performance problems.

  Your job: Stress that team members are responsible to each other for reducing conflicts. You can make that apparent by referring to the charter during subsequent team meetings.

- *A charter creates team identity.* Your teams' charter proclaims what the team stands for and how it accomplishes work. It also is a useful tool for getting new team members up to speed.

  Your job: Bring the members together and give them what they need (space, time, equipment) to work according to their charter.

Creating a Charter

The final charter should be a formal, typed document to which everyone on the team has easy access. Use a format that best suits your teams' needs. To help your teams create a charter, refer to the chart on the facing page for guidance. ➤

Section Description	Questions the Team Needs to Answer	How You Can Provide Guidance
Purpose Describes why a team exists. Defines how a team will deliver a product or provide a service.	• Why exactly does our team exist? • Who are our customers? • How is our team different/similar to others in this organization?	Distribute a copy of the organization's mission or vision statement before the chartering meeting. Ask teams how their purpose meshes with this vision.
Responsibilities Describes the responsibilities or outputs for which a team will be accountable.	• What do we have to do to accomplish the team's purpose? • What must we do to ensure that our product or service meets customer requirements?	Remind teams to refer to their Empowerment Schedule for tasks they will take on.
Boundaries Clarifies how much a team can do on its own and how much other people must be involved.	• What limits has management set for us? • What kinds of decisions can we make? • What kinds of decisions do we get approval for?	Check with your manager, design team, or steering committee on any parameters for the teams. (For example, most new teams spend about 15 percent of their time in meetings and in training.)
Ground Rules Defines acceptable and unacceptable behavior within the team.	• How will our team make decisions? • How will we resolve conflicts? • What was the worst team experience and what should be done to keep that from recurring?	• Find out what the norms are for other teams. • Suggest that the teams follow up on how well they are adhering to the ground rules in weekly team meetings. • Examine your idiosyncrasies—be prepared to let go of them.
Meetings Describes the time, frequency, and location of meetings.	• How often and how long will we meet? • Where and when will we meet? • How often during the New Team Phase?	Help your teams develop guidelines for typical agendas. (See page 85.)

Week 2
Productive team meetings

Conducting meetings is often one of the first responsibilities teams take on. Two common types of meetings they'll need your help with are (1) shift overlap meetings and (2) weekly team meetings.

Shift Overlap Meetings

These meetings, which last about 15 to 30 minutes after the shift, have many opportunities for coaching and team collaboration. Don't underestimate their usefulness! During these meetings the team can cover problems, priorities, errors and ideas for correcting them, or getting the product or service delivered. Even if your teams already have shift overlap meetings as well as shift change notes, work with them to develop an even more effective team-oriented process. Use the sample form at right to develop your own agenda.

The benefits of effective overlap meetings are:

- Reduced interpersonal tension.

- Improved coordination.

- Improved accountability.

Sample Shift Change Meeting Agenda

> ***Quality***—*5 minutes*
>
> *Opportunity to review performance against customer requirements*
>
> ***Schedule***—*5 minutes*
>
> *Status of product or service against delivery schedule; covering any bottlenecks*
>
> ***Problems during shift that next shift needs to know***—*3 minutes*
>
> *Backlogs, recurring problems, changes in priorities*
>
> ***Possible solutions to problems***—*7 minutes*
>
> *Joint brainstorming between team members*

PROVIDE COACHING HERE

Weekly Team Meetings and Sample Agendas

During the first six months, weekly team meetings often last one to two hours, focusing on technical training and team development. For the first three meetings, involve team members in helping you draw up agendas. It is critical that you find an appropriate balance between too little leadership (which results in drifting) and too much leadership (which causes the team to be dependent). Following are examples of three weekly team meeting agendas.

Meeting 1	Date:
Topic	**Time**
Technical Development	
Review equipment changes or movement	*30 minutes*
Review quality and productivity goals	*1 hour*
Team Development	
Discuss videos viewed or chapters read on teams	*15 minutes*
Work on team charter, especially operating guidelines	*1 hour*

Meeting 2	Date:
Topic	**Time**
Technical Development	
Review and agree on the cross-training plan	*30 minutes*
Assess how effective shift change meetings are and brainstorm improvements	*30 minutes*
Team Development	
Agree on basic guidelines for tasks in the Empowerment Schedule	*30 minutes*
Prepare agenda for the next meeting	*15 minutes*

Meeting 3	Date:
Topic	**Time**
Technical Development	
Review first month's performance against the baseline	*1 hour*
Brainstorm ways to improve performance	*30 minutes*
Team Development	
Check everyone's comfort with and clarity on new roles	*30 minutes*
Star point reports	*45 minutes*

Week 3
Creating accountability on your teams

One of the hallmarks of empowered teams is taking increased responsibility for their own leadership. In the beginning new teams need some structure or guidance to follow. You will want to provide that structure to keep them on the right track. A team that makes a false start is one that will give you problems in the future.

Making team members accountable for tasks and responsibilities is one way you can help employees become familiar with the new team system and its opportunities. Shared leadership means ownership and self-direction for the team—and increased comfort for you. For transfer of leadership responsibility to occur in a smooth and orderly manner, you need a plan.

Organize the responsibilities listed in your Empowerment Schedule by categories or groups of related tasks. (See example at right.) These categories will be the points of accountability and contact for team members. Each "star point" is an opportunity for someone to "own" that responsibility. This star point system is one of the most effective and efficient ways to share leadership responsibilities with your teams. If your steering committee or design team hasn't already done so, you can create a star point plan for your teams, using the space at right.

Empowerment Schedule Tasks	Star Point Category
Revise ISO 9000 procedures	*Quality*
Coordinate fire extinguisher checks	*Safety*
Schedule product changeovers	*Production*
Conduct safety audits	*Safety*
Call maintenance	*Maintenance*
Schedule maintenance	*Maintenance*
Debrief team on business status	*Communication*
Coordinate shift change	*Communication*
Cross-train on pump repair	*Maintenance*

Empowerment Schedule Tasks	Star Point Category

How the Star Concept Works

In the star point system, each team member is responsible for a point on the star for a predetermined period. Every three or four months, the start points rotate so that after one and a half to two years everyone on the team has had a chance to perform all the various leadership functions. You or a support professional coach and train each person on how to carry out that responsibility effectively. (The support professional would share information and explain what information he or she needs from the team.)

What star point categories best fit your teams' Empowerment Schedule? If you have more than five categories, use the inside points of the star to note the rest.

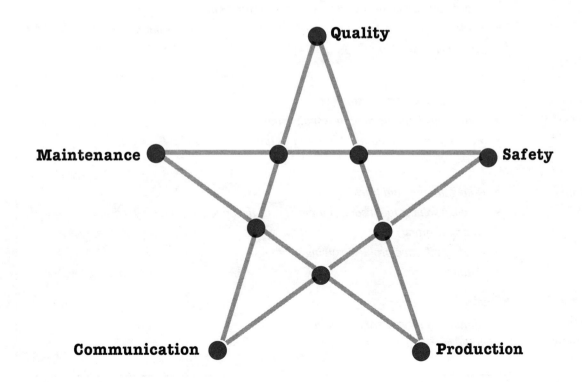

Week 4
Clarifying the star points

As with all new team roles it's very important to be clear about expectations. For this reason each star point needs a "job description" that clearly states responsibilities, goals, and available support. To create a job description, have your team members fill in the information for these five topics:

• The star point's purpose.

• A list of responsibilities.

• Measurement methods to gauge success.

• Skills and training the team member needs to succeed.

• Key support professionals or managers who can act as resources or consultants.

Sample Star Point Job Description

Quality Star Point

Purpose: *To coordinate the team's effort to ensure quality service.*

Responsibilities: • *Update customer service reports.*
     • *Review standard operating procedures biweekly with the team.*
     • *Collect and post response times.*
     • *Coordinate problem-solving meetings for error control.*
     • *Participate in cross-functional, problem-solving efforts that address service problems across teams.*

Measures of Success: • *Percentage of return customers.*
     • *Continuous improvement in response times.*
     • *Members' understanding of procedures and quality standards.*

Training Needed: • *Data gathering and tracking.*
     • *Problem-solving tool usage (Pareto charts, fishbone diagramming, variance control charting).*
     • *Leading effective problem-solving meetings.*
     • *Training others.*

Key Resources to Contact: *Pat Smith, Manager, Service Quality*
     Rich Wagner, Manager, Training

Your Next Step

Divide a team into smaller groups. Have each group develop job descriptions for a few star points. (Photocopy and distribute the form.) Remember: The responsibilities section should match your Empowerment Schedule. Include tasks from the schedule that teams will be handling by the end of one year.

After the job descriptions are written, review all of them as a team. Assign a volunteer to proofread the team's work for consistency. Review the polished job descriptions at the next team meeting.

Star Point Job Description Form

_____**Star Point**

Purpose:

Responsibilities:

Measures
of Success:

Training
Needed:

Key Resources
to Contact:

Notes. . .

Month 1

When to Call for Help

- Your manager insists that you proceed with teams without going through the team start-up process. Walk your manager through the start-up process. Talk about the benefits of working through the process (clear roles, coordination of work) as well as the consequences of not completing the process (unclear roles, fuzzy goals, chaotic processes, duplication of skills, etc.).

- Your team begins to exceed the allotted time for training. Ask yourself, Is this a problem for meeting our customer needs? If the answer is yes, reevaluate your training plan to make sure it's spaced over time and provided just in time.

If You Do Nothing Else . . .

1. Clarify your and team members' roles, even for the routine, unappealing tasks.

2. Begin work on a team charter.

3. Be clear about accountability.

Month at a Glance

MONDAY	TUESDAY	WEDNESDAY	THURSDAY	FRIDAY	SATURDAY/ SUNDAY
Review the team start-up process —30 minutes	Begin creating the team's charter —2 hours	Finalize the team's charter —2 hours			
Prepare for team meeting —45 minutes	Team meeting —2 hours				
	Team meeting —2 hours Identify star points —30 minutes				
Create star points job descriptions —2 hours	Team meeting —2 hours	Coach on star points with individual team members ← —6 hours	→ —6 hours	Polish the charter and distribute to internal customers and suppliers —30 minutes	

Time Budget

	Goal	Actual
Team coaching	40%	
Project work	10%	
Administrative	40%	
Personal development	10%	

Key Lessons

_____
_____
_____
_____
_____
_____
_____

Next Steps

_____
_____
_____
_____
_____
_____
_____

91

New Team Month 2

Notes. . .

Month 2

What to Expect

This month presents you with some new challenges and some new opportunities:

- Frequent technical cross-training will become necessary. Too often employees (and leaders) neglect cross-training because they are in a rush to take on more leadership tasks. You'll find that everyone needs to be cross-trained; this enables them to grasp the teams' technical processes and make good business decisions.

- You'll need patience as employees become accustomed to collaborating and to supporting each other as a team.

A big part of your job will be to motivate your employees to do their best. Part of that will come from sharing leadership responsibility. But there's more to it than that. You also will have to use the processes introduced this month to continually motivate team members. By doing so you will increase your teams' success.

Possible Concerns

My teams have bonded a little too well. They're hoarding equipment, keeping information from other teams, and generally becoming competitive. Now what do I do?

Often, employees who rarely spoke to each other before teams form such strong bonds that they become overzealous as a team. One way to address this overly competitive behavior is to review the overall business goals with your teams and reinforce the importance of cooperation among teams.

I was hoping the team setup would eliminate my repeat offenders—those employees who hand off work or errors to a few employees who carry the rest of the team. I still see the repeat offenders hanging back, waiting for someone else to fix their mistakes.

You might not see changes in employee work habits in the first two months. After all, these habits were developed over many years. Make sure you reinforce all attempts at collaboration and the importance of doing a quality job the first time. If you don't see improvement in another month, counsel the repeat offenders about their responsibilities to their fellow team members.

Your Focus This Month

This month you will focus on:

- Selecting team members for star points.

- Motivating your teams to help you make the change happen.

- Encouraging team members to work together.

- Building understanding through cross-training.

Week 1
Selecting team members for star points

Eventually, everyone will get a chance to rotate through all the star points. But in the beginning let teams assign the star points to members whose skills best match the responsibilities in each point.

Selecting people qualified for star points need not be difficult or complicated. Following is a sample chart developed by one team for placing five members in star points. They used the Skill Guide to complete the matrix and to decide who to assign to which star point.

Sample Star Point Skills

Team Member	Quality	Safety	HR	Finance	Communication	Choices
Linda	✔ ●	◖	⊕	⊕	◖	1. Quality 2. Communication
Bob	◔	●	✔ ●	⊕	⊕	1. HR 2. Quality
Ken	◖	◖	⊕	◖	✔ ◖	1. Communication 2. Safety
Terry	◖	◖	◖	✔ ◖	⊕	1. Finance 2. HR
Kate	◖	✔ ◔	◖	◖	⊕	1. Safety 2. HR

Skill Guide ⊕ Can describe this task, but has never done it.   ◖ Has performed this task alone.   ✔ Star point selection

◖ Has perormed this task with someone else.   ● Has trained others in this task.

Creating a Star Point Skills Grid

1. List the star points across the top of the grid and ask the team to agree on three or four responsibilities for each star point. Write those responsibilities under the appropriate heading.

2. Ask each team member to note his or her skill level for each star point, using the symbols displayed on page 94.

3. Ask each team member to choose which star point would be his or her first preference, and which the second preference. Remind them that everyone eventually will work in all the points.

4. Have the team match high-skill levels with the first and second choices. When more than one team member chooses the same point and both have at least performed this task with someone else, ask those members to agree on who will be first.

If your team has enough members, select a star point and a "star point in training"—someone who serves as an understudy or backup.

5. Rotate star points so that at least two people on the team have a chance to learn that star point each year.

Star points require coordination and training. Therefore, star points are best rotated every three to six months so the incumbent can learn and perform the required star point tasks. Not all star points are equal: Some star points (such as finance) will require more time for learning than others (such as housekeeping).

Week 2
Energizing new teams

It's important for the success of the change effort that you motivate other people to help you make the change happen. Think of what you can say or do that will inspire team members to take initiative and responsibility, learn new skills, and act on problems. If you're having difficulty coming up with ideas, think of someone (a manager, supervisor, peer) you have admired for his or her ability to work with people. This person might have been an exceptionally good motivator or coach. Identify characteristics or actions of someone you admire in the space provided on this page. Review the example for ideas.

Example

What did this person do that inspired you to do your best?	How did this person do that, and how often?
• *She asked questions that showed she spent time analyzing our situation.* • *She praised me when I performed well and wasn't afraid to straighten me out when I performed poorly.* • *She applied the same high standards she used on us to herself.*	• *She encouraged me by saying that my effort would lead to better performance.* • *She and I discussed the results and benefits that would come from improved performance.* • *She showed me how I was instrumental in making things happen in my department.*

Answer the following questions to describe an inspiring manager, peer, or supervisor:

1. **What did this person do that inspired me to do my best?**

2. **How did this person do that, and how often?**

Develop a Motivational Plan

The following motivational model will help you translate your ideas and best intentions into real actions that will have a positive impact on motivating your team members.

Valuable Outcomes

Determine the "attractive" outcomes for your team members.

Valued outcomes could include:

- A chance to work with peers.

- Working with customers.

- Seeing a task through to completion.

- More pay for skills used.

- Training opportunities.

Instrumental Tasks

Describe how the task (cross-training, rotation, meetings) is instrumental in obtaining the outcomes they value.

Descriptions could include:

- Cross-training leads to interaction with peers.

- Interpersonal skills training leads to opportunities to work with customers.

- Rotating jobs enables members to understand the whole process.

- Cross-training builds skills for which members may be compensated.

Positive Expectations

Build confidence that extra effort will lead to better performance and valued outcomes.

Create positive expectations by:

- Reinforcing team members who attempt to make an extra effort, whether successful or not.

- Discussing tasks with a can-do attitude.

- Reinforcing team members' abilities.

Team Member	Valued outcomes I can influence	Instrumental tasks I can effect	What I can do to build positive expectations
1. *Rich*	1. *Likes challenge*	1. *Ask Rich to develop our cross-training system.*	1. *Discuss how vital the cross-training system is to our team goals.*
2.	2.	2.	2.
3.	3.	3.	3.
4.	4.	4.	4.

Week 3
Sharing work in a team

When people share their expertise, ask questions, and offer ideas for solving problems, the quality of the work, product, or service is likely to improve. In addition, such give and take will increase each person's knowledge about the job and its processes. Simply dividing the work by the number of team members is not working in teams (although this approach might be an option during a crisis). However, some people will have trouble understanding how they can share their work on a daily basis. If you have that problem, share with your team members the following examples of successful team collaboration.

	Work Done Previously As Individuals	**How Team Members Share Work**
Sales Representatives	*Called on customers and prospects in their own territory.*	*Sales team assesses all the prospects and customers in a particular region and assigns people or pairs to accounts, based on the reps' skills and the customers' needs.*
Nurses	*Registered nurses (RNs) assessed patients, bathed patients, ordered and delivered medications, and oversaw charts for six patients.*	*RNs, licensed practical nurses (LPNs), and technicians jointly assess patients and then perform tasks based on their skill level for eight patients. The result: RNs spend more time with the patient and LPNs have a chance to learn clinical skills.*
Customer Service Specialists	*Highly skilled individuals worked on one type of customer account. They were not concerned about, or responsible for, different customers with similar types of service needs.*	*Team members who are familiar with the service needs of customers within the same geographical area are seated together so they can answer each other's telephone calls and plan ways to deal with tough service needs.*
Engineers	*Engineers worked alone on defining research project limits, deadlines, types of tests, equipment, and so forth.*	*Engineers with varying expertise and from different projects work as a team to define projects, types of tests, and so forth, sharing knowledge and expertise daily.*

What You Can Do

Ask yourself: What does someone do now that a team, working together, could do better? Review tasks in your group and consider what you can do to help team members complete a task that now is done independently by all team members. Write your ideas in this form. Some examples are provided.

Topics	How can I help increase the sharing of work?
<ul><li>*Assigning work.*</li><li>*Planning team meeting agenda focused on shared work.*</li><li>*Handling unusually high work loads.*</li></ul>	<ul><li>*Create and prominently post a work assignment board, emphasizing shared tasks.*</li><li>*Ask the team how they can better share their "tricks" or expertise.*</li><li>*Observe how the work is being done. Find out how people are filling in for each other or what would have to happen to increase everyone's ability to fill in for each other.*</li></ul>

Week 4

Building understanding through cross-training

You want to start tackling errors in products or services. But where to begin? Building understanding among the team members of what is required in each function is a good start. At this point you cannot expect that every team member can perform every function on the team. One hundred percent cross-training is a goal and not yet a reality. But it is important that everyone on the team understand each function's difficulties, how the functions are affected by and dependent on each other, the costs associated with bottlenecks, and more.

Where is your team on the understanding thermometer?

100%—Team members have spent time in each other's areas, can describe the steps to perform the functions, and work to prevent defects from occurring from one function to the next.

50%—Team members have spent time in each other's areas, but could not describe all the steps on command.

25%—Team members have not spent significant time in each other's areas.

Where You Come In

Following are some ideas for improving your team members' understanding of all the team functions:

- Group team members by pairs. Have them spend three hours a week shadowing another team in an area with which they are unfamiliar.

- Hold three to four two-hour meetings in which you walk the entire team from function to function. Have each "function expert" explain the steps, typical barriers, requirements from the preceding function, and so on.

- Create a floor plan that shows the entire operation from start to finish. Explain the steps, costs of problems, and requirements for each function in a three-hour team meeting. Ask team members to bring questions.

Developing a Cross-training Plan

Once you have a solid foundation of understanding, you can go on to actual cross-training. Cross-training is the key to building complete understanding of workplace functions among your team members. However, cross-training all team members in all tasks is not very practical or financially sound. It's not practical because it could take up to six months for a team member to become fully proficient in a task. It's not financially sound because it's not necessary that all the team members use all their skills at the same time.

Your job is to help the team separate the must-have training from the nice-to-have training. The activities on the following pages will help you do that. Part 1 shows you how to help your team differentiate between must-have and nice-to-have cross-training. Part 2 gives you a form for plotting and tracking the cross-training.

Part 1: Must-have vs. Nice-to-have Cross-training

To identify what cross-training your teams need to have, first determine the skills required so that the product or service meets your customers' requirements. What are the skills your group needs to use the most? In this example, a printing and distribution team created the following grid to identify the areas where cross-training would have the greatest impact. ("Touch time" refers to the period during which the team is actually working on or handling a product or service.)

Sample Cross-training Impact Chart

Major business functions required to meet customer needs during the last year	Accounts for what percent of our team's touch time on the product	Time needed to become competent in this function, and the level of difficulty
Develop print plates *Number of employees: 4*	*25 percent touch time*	*Nine months to learn 85 steps* *Level: Difficult*
Copying *Number of employees: 5*	*40 percent touch time*	*One month to learn eight steps* *Level: Simple*
Develop binders *Number of employees: 8*	*10 percent touch time*	*Four months to learn eight pieces of equipment* *Level: Moderately difficult*
Collation and tabs *Number of employees: 20*	*10 percent touch time*	*Two weeks to learn two pieces of equipment* *Level: Simple*
Warehousing and shipping *Number of employees: 12*	*15 percent touch time*	*Two months to learn how to pick and restock; one month to learn shipping* *Level: Simple*

Armed with this information, the organization decided that its cross-training priorities were copying, developing binders, and warehousing and shipping. It based its decision on these factors:

- Because they require less than six months to train and are easy or only moderately difficult to learn, cross-training in these skills would be practical.

- Together, these skills account for a significant amount of the team's touch time on the product (about 65 percent).

Doing Your Own

Working with your teams, complete the worksheet on page 102 to decide which of your teams' functions are cross-training priorities.

Continued on next page

Cross-training Planning Worksheet

Major business functions required to meet customer needs during the last year	Accounts for what percent of our team's touch time on the product	Time needed to become competent in this function, and the level of difficulty	Must-have or nice-to-have cross-training

How to Cross-train

To this point you have identified what to cross-train. Following are some fail-safe steps for how to make cross-training effective. Work with your training star point on these steps:

1. Provide classroom training with diagrams, checklists, or other job aids to explain the entire task. Ask the trainee to repeat what he or she learned.

2. Create a troubleshooting guide for common problems that can happen on the job. Include steps the trainee can follow to correct the problems.

3. Assign an on-the-job mentor for the trainee. The mentor should check with the trainee three times a day for the first two or three weeks. Set up meetings at which the trainee and experts can discuss how the cross-training is going.

4. Certify the trainee by asking him or her to perform the task on the job.

Part 2: Plotting the Cross-training

Have your team members complete this cross-training grid. When completed they will be able to see in one glance where their skills are and where they need training. Update the grid as team members complete training.

Team Functions / Team Members									
	⊕	⊕	⊕	⊕	⊕	⊕	⊕	⊕	⊕
	⊕	⊕	⊕	⊕	⊕	⊕	⊕	⊕	⊕
	⊕	⊕	⊕	⊕	⊕	⊕	⊕	⊕	⊕
	⊕	⊕	⊕	⊕	⊕	⊕	⊕	⊕	⊕
	⊕	⊕	⊕	⊕	⊕	⊕	⊕	⊕	⊕
	⊕	⊕	⊕	⊕	⊕	⊕	⊕	⊕	⊕

The completion of the circle indicates the degree of proficiency at each task:

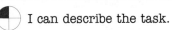 I can describe the task.

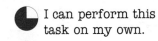 I can perform this task on my own.

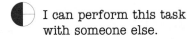 I can perform this task with someone else.

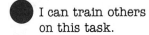 I can train others on this task.

Notes. . .

Month 2

When to Call for Help

- You have questions about whether or not cross-training is a problem for your union contract or government regulations. Ask a union leader to work with you to revise the contract with respect to cross-training. Consult with the appropriate authorities.

- You find that team members have difficulty sharing the work because of "turf" issues. Consider training the group as a team in a few key skills.

- Some members refuse to accept star point responsibilities. State explicitly in the team charter that members must assume such responsibilities. You might also want to ask successful leaders how they have handled this situation.

If You Do Nothing Else . . .

1. Develop a plan for motivating and energizing team members.

2. Make sure you address team development issues as well as production issues in team meetings.

3. Reinforce team members who try to gain new skills or responsibilities weekly.

Month at a Glance

MONDAY	TUESDAY	WEDNESDAY	THURSDAY	FRIDAY	SATURDAY/ SUNDAY
	Select and match team members to star points —2 hours		Compare my teams' charter with those of other shifts/depts.; look for consistency —1 hour		
	Team meeting —2 hours	Devise ways to motivate the team members and start two tactics today —2 hours			
Assess whether team members share work; suggest ways to increase sharing —2 hour	Team meeting —2 hours			Motivate employess —2 hours	
	Team meeting —1 hours		Special team meeting to develop our teams' cross-training plans —2 hour	Discuss cross-training plan with my manager —30 minutes	

Time Budget

	Goal	Actual
Team coaching	50%	
Project work	10%	
Administrative	30%	
Personal development	10%	

Key Lessons

_____

_____

_____

_____

_____

_____

Next Steps

_____

_____

_____

_____

_____

_____

New Team Month 3

Notes. . .

Month 3

What to Expect

Most teams pass through four stages as they develop into fully mature, empowered teams. In the first stage, Getting Started, team members get to know each other's capabilities and limits as well as the scope of their jobs. In the second stage, Going in Circles, teams handle the frustration that comes with taking wrong turns and making mistakes. By the third stage, Getting on Course, team members are more comfortable with each other and their responsibilities, and can see that they are making some progress. It's in the final stage, Full Speed Ahead, that teams start to achieve their goals using all the knowledge and skills they've gained since the rocky beginning.

4. Full Speed Ahead

1. Getting Started

3. Getting on Course

2. Going in Circles

At this point in the transition, your teams are either in the Getting Started stage or the beginning of the Going in Circles stage. Team members might be excited about the change, but they're also anxious. They're struggling with understanding expectations—theirs and yours—or how they're supposed to achieve their goals. Still, there might be some real progress you can share with team members. For instance, by the end of this month, you should see team members who are committed to working in teams as well as improvements in morale, communication, trust, and participation.

Assessing Progress

You can gauge a team's progress by conducting a regularly scheduled "check-up." Share the information you get from these assessments with the teams. Specifically tell them what they've been doing that will move them forward and what they've been doing that holds them back.

To help them get back on track, it's a good idea at this point to have the teams review their charters. Now that they know more about teams and what's expected of them, they might want to revise their charters to better reflect current reality.

Possible Concerns

When I get to work in the morning, I'm sometimes faced with unwelcome surprises left by a team from the day before. Just when I think the team members clearly understand what we agreed to, the next day I find that they either misunderstood or changed the decision.

Make sure you document the agreement or decision and display it where it can be read, say on the team's white board or shift change notes. It's also a good idea to check team members' understanding of an agreement by having them summarize it.

Our teams have had some initial success. They certainly prefer working in teams over working as individuals. But there's always somebody who will ask, What benefit do teams have for our company? What kind of answers will put these questions to rest?

One approach is to put the move to teams in the context of what is happening within your industry. Ask your managers or another organization resource for information on your organization's market share. Draw a graph or chart (such as the example) to illustrate how the organization fits in with the industry.

In this example the organization is not growing as fast as the industry as a whole. It shows that there is potential for growth if the organization institutes major changes, such as implementing teams. This kind of change would allow employees at all levels to develop new ways of doing things to meet current and future customer needs.

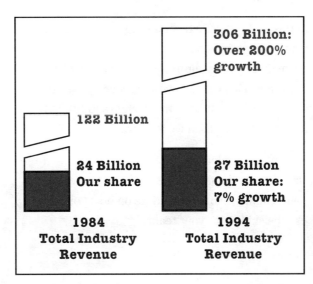

306 Billion: Over 200% growth

122 Billion

24 Billion Our share

27 Billion Our share: 7% growth

1984 Total Industry Revenue

1994 Total Industry Revenue

Your Focus This Month

This month you will work on the following areas as your teams become more familiar with their new roles and responsibilities:

- Building your skills—continued.

- Creating a team business plan.

- Giving the team a "health check."

- Celebrating and recognizing your team members' hard work.

Week 1

Building your skills—continued

Think of the skills you need to manage or implement a new project, such as adding new equipment, products, or services. To do any of those activities well you need a high level of skill. You'll also need this same degree of skill to lead and manage organizational change and the team implementation.

In this early stage of team development, you face some new and unusual challenges. Also, you're trying to grow in your new role. Practicing the following skills will help you (1) coach your teams and help them adjust to the change and (2) improve your skills in working with teams.

Review the key learning points for each of the three skill areas and check those you want to include in your training. Note some ideas on how you can use the skills with your teams.

1. Rescuing Difficult Meetings

- Recognize unproductive patterns of interaction.

- Intervene while maintaining the other person's self-esteem.

- Reach high-quality decisions more quickly.

What I can do to rescue meetings that are in trouble:

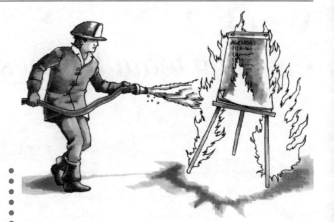

2. Encouraging Initiative

- Create a more challenging and satisfying work environment.

- Develop creative suggestions.

- Ask questions that help team members develop their own ideas.

What I can do to encourage initiative:

3. Coaching for Success

- Identify ways to enhance individual and team performance.

- Provide opportunities for team members to develop their skills, either with challenging assignments or new responsibilities.

- Provide feedback on individual and team performance.

What I can do to coach team members to succeed:

Week 2

Creating team business plans

New team leaders often struggle with how to keep teams focused and accountable for their performance. One of the best approaches is to develop a team business plan. You and your teams, working together, should develop a team business plan that:

- Aligns the team with the organization's business plan.

- Encourages the team to monitor how it's doing against its goals.

- Keeps the team focused on its priorities.

Sample Team Business Plan

Organization Goals	Team Focus and Baseline Data	Team Goals	Individual Actions
Safety • *No more than five recordables throughout the facility*	• *Currently have no recordables* • *New hires need safety training*	• *Zero recordables in the next year* • *Give new employees safety training during first week*	*Pat:* Conduct safety training quarterly *Don:* Restock safety equipment weekly *Mary:* Eliminate on-the-job accidents
Quality • *Reduce rejects by 10 percent*	*Current reject rate is 15 percent*	*Reduce rejects by 5 percent*	*Pat:* ⎫ • *Learn to set specifications with* *Don:* ⎬ *greater accuracy* *Mary:* ⎭ • *Inspect product before it goes out*
Employee Involvement • *Increase work teams' sense of ownership* • *Make more use of employees' skills*	*Star point functioning:* • *Each team member is learning one star point* • *Increase team members' star point skills*	*All team members will rotate to at least one star point within the next six months*	*Pat:* Train Don as a backup on quality star point this quarter *Don:* Document new safety procedures for the next star point to use *Mary:* Meet with the facility accountant to discuss transition plan for the next star point

Ready, Set, Go!

Working with your teams, create business plans that they can use to maintain their enthusiasm and that you can use to encourage their initiative. Use the suggested worksheet on this page, or create one of your own design. Follow these steps:

1. Collect the organization's goals.

2. Interview customers about their needs.

3. Select team focus areas based on the organization's goals and customer feedback.

4. Develop an action plan for each focus area. Identify team members who can be responsible for each part of the plan.

Organization Goals	Team Focus and Baseline Data	Team Goals	Individual Actions

Week 3
Taking the teams' temperature—Part 1

Every team can benefit from a thorough examination every once in a while. In fact, now is a good time to do a formal evaluation of your teams and their development.

Why Do an Evaluation?

There are at least two very good reasons why you should evaluate your teams' performance now:

1. Many teams develop ineffective interaction patterns or poor decision-making techniques in their first few months. Unless you conduct an evaluation now, these problems might go undetected until the team has worked together for some time—making resolution that much more difficult.

2. Because new teams often focus on the technical aspects of their work, they need help focusing on team development.

What Should I Evaluate?

You will want to evaluate team performance in six factors that are directly related to team success:

- *Purpose* is the reason for the team's existence: its direction, identity, and focus. A team with a purpose can concentrate on important issues and direct its time and resources toward specific goals. Purpose answers the question, Why have we formed a team?

- *Process* is the established methods, systems, and procedures a team uses to accomplish its work. Process can be a series of steps or operations that a team uses to reach a goal or complete a task, or it can refer to the technical and interpersonal skills people need to do their jobs.

- *Communication* is the exchange of ideas, information, and feelings in a way that respects others and acknowledges their need to be included and involved. It is more than just talking.

- *Commitment* is harder to observe than the other factors because it's such a personal feeling. Consider a team committed when its members believe they own a situation, solution, or system.

- *Involvement* means sharing talents, skills, and knowledge with people in and outside the team. Involvement builds commitment.

- *Trust* is when team members know they can rely on each other. It's a willingness to believe in the intentions and motivations of people outside the team. Imagine how paralyzing it would be to work every day with people you don't trust.

How Do I Evaluate the Team?

At this stage team members should rate the team's development on items that measure the six factors of team success. Special team development kits are available for this purpose. (See the map of books and training materials at the end of this guide.) These kits help to pinpoint progress on the six factors as well as identify the team's stage of development (Getting Started, Going in Circles, Getting on Course, Full Speed Ahead).

Without such a kit, try leading a team through a force-field analysis of what's working and not working on each factor. Follow these steps to complete a force-field analysis such as the one illustrated on this page.

Creating a force-field analysis

1. Label six boxes (one for each factor) and use a plus sign to designate the left-side items working in your team's favor and a minus sign to designate the right-side items preventing your team from making progress. Split the two sides with a vertical line, dividing them equally.

2. For each factor, identify the positive aspects and write them on the left side under the plus sign. Draw an arrow toward the middle for each aspect. Use thick or long arrows for the most important positive aspects.

3. For each factor identify the negative aspects and write them on the right side under the minus sign. Draw an arrow toward the middle for each aspect. Use thick or long arrows for the most important negative aspects.

4. Discuss what actions you and your team can take to work on improving negative aspects and to take advantage of positive aspects of the factor.

Sample Force-field Analysis

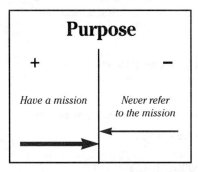
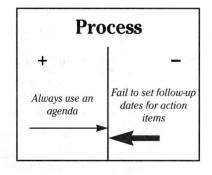
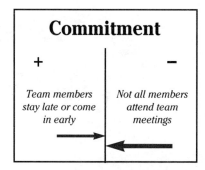
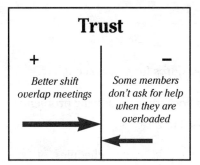
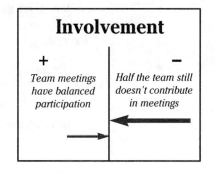
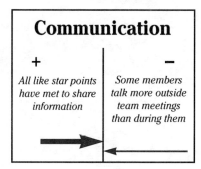

Continued on next page

Using What You Learned

This analysis is particularly helpful in identifying those areas in which your teams are weak. Following are some suggestions for what you and your teams can do in each factor that would improve performance.

Purpose

- Relate goals to the organization's mission statement.

- Refer to the teams' charters when considering new tasks.

- Revise roles and short-term goals as projects and tasks change.

- Question assignments that don't contribute to long-term goals.

Process

- Establish procedures for solving conflicts.

- Establish and post steps for solving problems or implementing new ideas.

- Use flip charts, blackboards, schedules, or planners during meetings.

- Seek training in problem-solving, meeting, and interaction processes.

Communication

- Avoid jumping from topic to topic in meetings.

- Explore ideas; don't judge them.

- Include each other in decisions, updates, and problem solving.

- Help team members learn to clarify information they don't understand.

Involvement

- Encourage quiet team members to contribute.

- Distribute work evenly.

- Encourage and build on other people's ideas and initiatives.

- Try to balance individual needs and skills with team roles.

Commitment

- Work at meeting deadlines.

- Help teams live up to their agreements.

- Create realistic expectations of yourself and others.

- Make tasks rewarding and challenging.

- Clearly define benefits for individuals and teams.

Trust

- Encourage teams to support and praise each other.

- Keep sensitive information confidential.

- Discourage gossip and unfair criticism.

- Express appreciation for other people's skills and initiatives.

- Avoid hidden agendas; keep goals out in the open.

Week 4
Celebrating success

Early in the move to teams, people appreciate being recognized and rewarded for their efforts—and the teams' first three-month review provides the perfect opportunity. Most teams will have made some progress by this time.

At this point stinginess is not a virtue! Find ways to recognize your team members for all their hard work. Team celebrations can go further than the recognition itself. They increase interaction among team members and reduce barriers between them and management.

A cautionary note: While celebrations have great value, if held too often or on a regular schedule (as if they were just another part of the new team structure) their impact and usefulness are weakened. Moreover, team celebrations don't always have to be gala events. An impromptu 15-minute "mini celebration" to recognize hard work or achieving a new milestone also can be effective.

Examples of Team Celebrations

- A radio repair facility gives teams a few hours off two Fridays a month when the team produces its output goals two weeks in a row.

- Team members at a computer company's software support center used a team bonus to purchase books that all employees could use. The books were put in a team library.

- To celebrate exceeding their productivity and quality goals, all 25 technicians in a steel mill took a one-day hunting trip.

- All the sales managers in one region got together to cook and serve dinner to the top-producing sales and service teams.

For your teams . . .

1. Ask your teams how they would like to celebrate their progress. Write their ideas in this space.

2. What ideas do you want to suggest to celebrate their success. Write your ideas below.

When to Call for Help

- Teams don't know enough about the business to develop goals or complete the business plan. Ask a manager, customer, or salesperson to talk about critical business issues with you and your teams.

- You run out of ideas to improve your teams' performance. Talk with successful team leaders; get their ideas.

- You need a neutral party to give you an objective view of your teams' progress. Consider recruiting someone who doesn't have a vested interest in your work processes.

- You want to make a big splash at a team celebration. Invite a vice president or key manager to talk to your teams about how teams are benefitting the company.

If You Do Nothing Else . . .

1. Involve your team in creating a business plan.

2. Check the teams' "health."

3. Celebrate your teams' successes to create a sense of accomplishment and pride within the team.

Month at a Glance

MONDAY	TUESDAY	WEDNESDAY	THURSDAY	FRIDAY	SATURDAY/ SUNDAY
	Tell my team what's happening in unit/organization —1 hour Team meeting —1 hour		Attend leader training —4 hours		
	Team meeting —1 hour	Provide technical coaching on the cross-training matrix —1 hour	Create the team's business plan —2½ hours	Attend leader training —4 hours	
Explain/Administer team check up —2 hours Schedule check-up interviews —30 minutes	Team meeting —1 hour Debrief my training with the team —1 hour	Coach star points —2 hours	Assess progress on our baseline —1 hour Plan for a team celebration —1 hour	Provide technical training on the cross-training grid —2 hourr	
Ask how the star points are working out —1 hour	Team meeting —1 hour Debrief the check-up results —1 hour		Team Celebration —2 hours	Debrief check-up with my manager —1 hour	

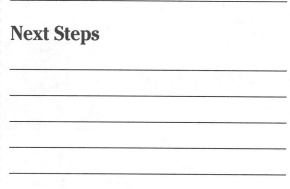

Time Budget

	Goal	Actual
Team coaching	50%	
Project work	10%	
Administrative	30%	
Personal development	10%	

Key Lessons

_____
_____
_____
_____
_____
_____
_____
_____

Next Steps

_____
_____
_____
_____
_____
_____
_____
_____

New Team Month 4

Notes. . .

Month 4

What to Expect

By now your teams are learning how to deal with their new and expanded responsibilities. It is probably a time of some confusion. They might be setting unrealistic goals, relying too much on one person or focusing on a task or goal, not on how to get it done. All this means that your teams are in the Going in Circles stage of team development.

4. Full Speed Ahead

1. Getting Started

3. Getting on Course

2. Going in Circles

You're probably feeling a sense of accomplishment and relief that your teams are past the Getting Started stage. But, at the same time, you and your teams are facing a whole new set of challenges. This month you'll be helping your teams get back on course by providing them with coaching and helping them focus on the overall business plan.

Also, this month you will want to keep your manager informed on how well your teams are meeting their business goals.

Possible Concerns

My manager hasn't been in touch with my teams. After we established our vision, he got busy with out-of-town work. I'm concerned that he'll underestimate the hard work we've put into making the teams work.

It's easy for people outside your team to underestimate all the work you and your team members have done. You can help avoid this misunderstanding by keeping your manager informed of your initial progress and the steps that have gotten you there. Send regular updates via voice mail or fax if your manager is frequently out of the office on business trips.

How long is too long for a team to be going in circles? When should I take formal action to get the team on course?

It's natural to worry that a team is spinning out of control. Generally, teams should not be in the Going in Circles stage for more than three or four months. If you tried the tips recommended in this guide and you still have communication, trust, participation, or personality problems, consider changing the members of a team.

Your Focus This Month

During the next few weeks you and your teams will be working on:

- How you can share more of your old role with team members.

- Building your teams' skills—continued.

- How to track business plan progress.

- Keeping your manager up to date.

Week 1
Sharing more of your old role

You've worked through sharing the first few leadership tasks, the cross-training plan, and the business plan. Now it's time to ask: Are my teams ready to take on additional responsibilities? Complete the following steps to start sharing more of your responsibilities with team members.

Step 1

Use an Empowerment Schedule (see example on page 11) as a guide for what to hand to teams next. At this point in the move to teams, you should have handed off about 15 percent of your responsibilities. Remember to use the questions in Preteam Month 5, Week 2 (see page 59). Use the formula below to calculate your progress.

$$\frac{\text{Number of tasks successfully handed to teams}}{\text{Total number of tasks on the Empowerment Schedule}} = \textbf{15\%}$$

If you are below the 15 percent guideline, ask yourself why that is so. Be sure you're not succumbing to any of these common excuses:

- "I have the background and experience, so I can do it better."

- "It will take the team too much time, and I can do it faster."

- "This assignment has high visibility with top management, so I'll do it and look good."

- "This is a risky decision, so I'm on the line."

- "I enjoy doing this too much myself to let the teams do it now."

Step 2

Ask your teams what they would like to do in the next three months. Identify those tasks that will require some coaching on your part. These typical next-step tasks might be:

- Leading team meetings.

- Keeping time and attendance.

- Assigning members to jobs.

- Making work schedules.

- Asking employees to work overtime.

- Contacting other departments directly for materials.

Step 3

Sometimes you will need to back off from coaching. Other times you will have to jump in right away to keep the teams from making mistakes, going in the wrong direction, or wasting time and effort. Deciding when to back off or jump in are among the most difficult judgment calls new leaders have to make. But knowing how to gauge when your help as a coach is needed and not needed will make a big difference in your effectiveness as a leader of new teams.

You should back off when:	You should jump in when:
• The team has clear goals and objectives.	• Objectives and goals are ambiguous or nonexistent.
• The team uses an agreed-upon process to gather data and generate solutions.	• The team regularly runs into dead ends, gets sidetracked, or begins to shut down.
• The team has assigned someone to monitor the process.	• The team charges ahead, that is, team members jump to conclusions or agree on a solution before gathering the information they need to make a good decision.
• The team is struggling with different solutions but is learning something valuable by doing so.	• The team hasn't discussed an issue fully.
• The team's solution wouldn't be your first choice, but you think it is viable.	• The team's solution overlooks key elements of the situation, making it unworkable.

Week 2

Turbocharged team skills: Building skills—continued

If your teams are like other new teams, difficulties are cropping up between team members. Are you beginning to see any of these problems?

- Team members have difficulty reaching a consensus quickly.

- Meetings stray over the budgeted time limit.

- People reveal their feelings after team meetings rather than in the meeting.

- Conflicts erupt between people who are jockeying to be informal leaders.

- Some team members, who are more interested in showing off than in teaching a task, are ineffectual trainers.

If any of these sound familiar, don't panic. Your teams simply need training in a new set of skills if they are to develop and advance as a team.

A New Set of Skills

Review the following skills and their key learning points. Check the appropriate box to indicate whether your teams use these points effectively now or whether they need to attend some training.

	Currently Use These Skills Effectively	Need More Training and Practice
1. Reaching Agreement Quickly		
• Use tools to narrow down ideas.	☐	☐
• Work effectively toward consensus.	☐	☐
• Develop criteria so that decisions meet business needs.	☐	☐
2. Coaching Others		
• Identify ways to enhance an individual's performance.	☐	☐
• Encourage team members to develop their skills in difficult assignments or new responsibilities.	☐	☐
• Provide feedback on individual performance.	☐	☐

	Currently Use These Skills Effectively	Need More Training and Practice
3. Resolving Conflict		
• Help others recognize and avoid potential conflicts.	☐	☐
• Help plan how to handle on-the-job conflicts.	☐	☐
• Identify shared goals to help resolve conflicts.	☐	☐
4. Supporting Others		
• Create a supportive work environment.	☐	☐
• Help others accomplish new tasks and meet challenges.	☐	☐
• Reinforce fellow team members' accomplishments.	☐	☐

Week 3

Eye appeal: Visual progress tracking

After you and your teams have identified team goals, you need to create a way in which the teams can track their progress at a glance. Following are examples of how three companies tracked progress.

Tracking Method	How It Was Done
A beer manufacturer uses an electric sign to display the quantity produced by the team on the previous day.	*The communication star point team member enters the data in the computer every day.*
Teams at a high-tech electronics manufacturing facility track daily units produced, number of out-of-spec units, and more on a white board that is kept in front of each team's area. #of shipments delivered on time — Baseline — Goal — Performance — Official Team Start-up — Week of July 20	*One team member comes in 15 minutes early each day to update the information board.*
A team at a customer service center electronically tracks the number of calls handled and the average length of each call.	*The team's service coordinator devised a program so that the entire team would see minute-to-minute changes in these numbers in a separate window at the top of their computer screen. She also prints out the weekly averages and posts them on the team bulletin board.*

Use the space on this page to sketch out your and your team members' ideas on how to track progress. Keep the following in mind while developing your tracking method:

- Make sure teams track indicators that are stated in a positive way. For example, they should be tracking the number of accurate shipments, not the number of inaccurate shipments. Tracking good news and successes is not only more motivating, it's more fun.

- Reinforce the importance of tracking by locating the chart or graph in a prominent place so everyone can see it easily. Discuss it daily or weekly with your team. People won't take time to update the visual if they think no one is interested in it.

- Let other managers know about the tracking chart so they can use the data.

What do you need to track?	How will you do it?

Week 4
Checkpoint #4: Staying in touch

Team Progress Review Meeting Notes

One way to keep your manager interested in your teams is to schedule an update and get him or her involved in the teams' progress. Be sure to:

- Show intiative by coming prepared with a few ideas.

- Ask for help with your problem areas.

- Ask for feedback about what you could be doing more—or less—of.

Once you've met with your manager, be sure to let your teams know what was discussed.

Agenda	Meeting Preparation Notes
8:00 Major tasks the team has been working on New responsibilities/decisions	Behavior/attitude changes: Productivity or quality changes:
8:20 External barriers impeding team progress	My ideas for removing these barriers:
8:40 Internal barriers impeding team progress	My ideas for removing these barriers:
9:00 How I have been spending my time What is working well with my new role What has **not** been working well with my new role that I would like to improve	My ideas about what I should be doing in the next few months: Your ideas for what I should be doing:

9:15 Resources I need from my manager to improve team functioning:
   • More technical training time
   • Manager spends more time with the team
	How much? By when?

9:30 End of meeting To-do list	Summarize conclusions.

How Did It Go?

Evaluate your meeting with your manager by answering the following questions.

- Was the meeting with your manager productive and successful? Cite some specific results.

- How did you feel when you left?

- What topics would you stress during your next meeting?

- How did your manager react to your teams' progress? To your ideas for overcoming barriers?

- What will you tell the team as a result of this meeting?

- Discuss review meetings with other leaders. Did they do something effective that you could use next time?

Notes. . .

Month 4

When to Call for Help

- A team has a performance or personality problem and you believe you need to move a team member to another team or department. Address this problem with the team, using your charter and ground rules. Try to get all team members to commit to living by the charter and to discuss the implications if they can't or won't.

- You want to arrange more recognition for the team and to present your initial team results to an audience of high-level managers. Ask your manager how he or she thinks this could be done most effectively.

- You discover that some of your team members have learning or reading disabilities. Contact your human resources department for assistance.

If You Do Nothing Else . . .

1. Have a progress review meeting with your manager.

2. Think of new challenges for your teams; transfer at least one new responsibility.

3. Reinforce team members' use of skills they learned in training.

Month at a Glance

MONDAY	TUESDAY	WEDNESDAY	THURSDAY	FRIDAY	SATURDAY/ SUNDAY
Plan new tasks to share with the teams —2 hours	Team meeting —1 hour	Hold a review session with star points —6 hours	Begin sharing new tasks —1 hour		
Team member skills training —4 hours	Track progress on the baseline; ask the teams for tracking ideas —2 hours		Coach team members to take on one new task ←——————→ —2 hours	—2 hours	
Review tracking boards —30 minutes	Team meeting —1 hour	Review my skills training manuals —30 minutes	Share another new task with the teams —1 hour	Coach a skeptical employee —30 minutes	
Provide technical assistance on the cross-training matrix —1 hour	Plan for the progress meeting with my manager —1 hour	Reinforce team member skills learned in training —30 minutes	Review tracking boards —30 minutes	Meet with my manager —1¹/² hours Debrief the meeting —30 minutes	

Time Budget

	Goal	Actual
Team coaching	50%	
Project work	10%	
Administrative	30%	
Personal development	10%	

Key Lessons

_____

_____

_____

_____

_____

Next Steps

_____

_____

_____

_____

_____

New Team Month 5

Notes. . .

Month 5

What to Expect

Teams are often still going in circles at this point. This happens because they're still getting adjusted to working together, and they're taking on new, more difficult tasks. This stormy period in teams' development will be prolonged if the team members have to adjust to new members, if they don't have skills in managing conflict, or if you solve all their problems for them.

As the teams take on more responsibility, the barriers they bump into become more challenging. You might find that this requires more coaching from you and other support groups.

In the midst of all this, you should take time to enjoy the sense of accomplishment as you and your teams overcome the new barriers.

Possible Concerns

Coaching is fine when team members listen. What if a team member needs coaching but won't pay attention to what I have to say?

This problem tends to occur in organizations with low trust levels and a record of poor management-labor relations. One manufacturing facility handled the situation this way: They developed a job description that specifies what it means to be a team member. It also states that team members must be open to coaching and includes the possible consequences of not adhering to the agreement.

What if I'm still afraid to take a real stand for the teams? After all, aren't they more responsible for problems now than I am?

Don't be afraid to take a stand supporting teams. Expect that some people inside and outside your department will challenge the move to teams. Listen to their concerns, doubts, and yes, ridicule—but don't be a fence sitter. Take a stand in favor of teams and stick with it. If you fail to do so, people:

- Won't value what you say.

- Might think the move to teams is only a fad.

- Will suspect you have a hidden agenda or that you really have no faith in the move yourself.

Ask yourself, Am I doing or saying something that causes people to doubt my commitment to teams? You should not:

- Make jokes to your peers about teams.

- Neglect to attend training yourself.

- Keep quiet when confronted by someone who disapproves of or disparages the team effort.

At the same time, you can ask yourself, How can I demonstrate my support for teams? You should:

- Be optimistic about potential team results.

- Talk with team members or peers often and ask them how they are doing.

- Show compassion for those who are struggling to change.

- Show fierce conviction that your teams will succeed.

- Share your positive thoughts about the vision for teams.

Your Focus This Month

You'll make real progress this month because you will be:

- Checking the teams' progress toward becoming more self-directed.

- Hosting a discussion on how the business plan is progressing.

- Breaking down barriers with other departments, shifts, or units.

- Giving the teams more challenging decision-making situations.

Week 1

Are your teams becoming more self-directed?

Checking Progress

Do you know where your teams are in their development? If not, you will want to check their progress now. Look for examples of behavior that, if not stopped now, could leave your teams with some bad, hard-to-break habits. Checking now also will let you, your team members, and your manager know about progress or where corrections need to be made. Follow these instructions to complete the form on page 135. The finished form will give everyone an easy-to-read team progress report.

Step 1

List the Empowerment Schedule tasks for the first three months.

Step 2

Ask the team members and other leaders to rate team competency on the tasks they have assumed during the last few months. Add your own ratings. Use this rating scale:

1 = Team members have taken responsibility for this task in name only. The supervisor still makes the decisions and coordinates activities around this task.

2 = Team members make some decisions around this task but rely on the leader for coaching, support, and sometimes, approval.

3 = The team makes many, if not most, of the decisions around this task, relying on the leader as an internal resource and, occasionally, for guidance or approval. Task responsibilities are shared.

4 = The team makes all of the decisions needed to complete this task with 100 percent accuracy and rarely, if at all, relies on the supervisor.

All ratings for all tasks should average at least a 3. If your teams rate below average (2 or less), refer to the coaching section in Preteam Month 5, Week 2 for ideas on how to address below average ratings. If your team is above a 3, celebrate!

Empowerment Schedule Tasks	Competency Ratings		
	Team	Other Leaders	My Ratings
1.			
2.			
3.			
4.			
5.			
6.			
7.			
8.			
9.			
10.			
11.			
12.			
13.			
14.			
15.			
16.			
17.			
18.			
19.			
20.			

Week 2
Discussing progress on the business plan

It's been two months since you helped the teams develop their own business plans. Now it's time to involve them in assessing their progress. Plan a meeting with the teams to discuss progress on the business plan. Include these topics on your agenda:

- Compare team performance to the agreed-upon objectives. (A plan for doing that follows.)

- Recognize team and individual strengths. (More on this next week.)

- Agree on ways to improve performance that fell short of the objectives.

- Emphasize continued improvement and development.

- Find ways for team members to evaluate data to enhance their understanding and sense of ownership of the business.

Presenting the Facts

There are a number of ways to track progress on the business plan. You might consider using this system, which was developed by a large chemical films manufacturer in Connecticut.

Step 1

Have team members commit to tracking one or two team goals; for instance, one member would track quality goals (reducing rejects), another safety goals (reducing the number of recordables), another team development (increasing the leadership task for each member), and so on.

Step 2

Advise the team members on how they can present their findings to the whole team. Help them prepare for their presentations by asking these questions:

1. What trend does the data show?

2. How close to the goal are we?

3. What steps could the team take to improve progress to the goal?

Step 3

Have each team member prepare a graphic representation of the data (see example below). At the meeting give each team member about 10 minutes to present the data and discuss the results with the team.

Sample Goal-Tracking Graph

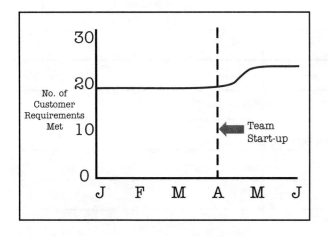

Summarize Overall Progress

Lead a discussion in the team meeting that summarizes the data just presented. Have team members discuss these questions:

- Is the team on target for meeting its goals?

- What percentage of the goals have been met?

- What actions will have the biggest impact on reaching a goal and on long-term teamwork?

After the discussion have the members start coordinating and implementing improvements that will help the teams reach their goals. Be careful not to take responsibility for action. Let the team members assume responsibility for what the team agreed to do.

Team Public Relations

This is a good time for the team to "blow its own horn." Its successes should not be a secret. Discuss with the teams ways to convey to the organization at large any initial successes. Consider doing the following. Add your and your teams' ideas to this short list.

- Submit a brief article to the organization's newsletter. Include a photograph of your team plus a description of your product or service.

- Make your progress an agenda item for your manager to discuss at his or her next staff meeting.

Week 3
Fostering interdependence

At this point in your teams' development, team members might be developing internal cohesiveness, sometimes by competing with or badmouthing other teams. It's your job to help them out of this state of independence to one of interdependence with other groups.

Use the following diagram to identify the other key groups your team interacts with:

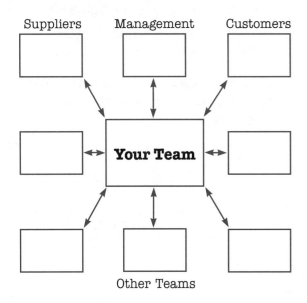

Complete the form below to rate the state of your teams' current relationship with these key groups using this scale:

1 = openly hostile toward this group

2 = tolerates but doesn't really understand this group

3 = understands and appreciates this group

Key Teams, Shifts, or Support Groups	Relationship (1, 2, or 3)

Planning Your Approach

Other leaders have used several approaches to break down the barriers between their teams and other units. Review the following ideas and add some of your own strategies.

1. Meet with other groups to identify a common problem; form a **joint problem-solving team.**

2. Host an **open house** for other groups to tour (and better understand) your area.

3. Meet with the other groups and **discuss expectations** and requirements of each other.

4. Ask both groups to **rate each other's performance.**

5. Have members of the two groups **swap jobs** for a specified time.

6. Invite members of the other group to your **team meetings.**

Now match these strategies to the groups with which your team has a poor relationship (groups with a rating of 1 or 2).

Group	Rating	Strategy	By When

Week 4
Providing more challenging decisions

It's not unusual for teams to get into a tug-of-war with their leaders over who is making what decisions. Often the teams are arguing for more autonomy, while leaders believe they need to be more involved in the decisions. At this point you might find that some of the decisions that need to be clarified have either slipped by your Empowerment Schedule or are not "meaty" enough to satisfy your team. One way to clarify roles, and to give your team members greater responsibility, is described at right.

Step 1

Ask your teams to think about all the decisions that will need to be made in the next month. Have them write down their ideas for later reference.

Step 2

With the team members, identify a high-risk decision (one that affects people outside your area, involves capital expenditures exceeding $10,000, affects the safety of others, etc.) and a low-risk decision (made every day within your department or work group).

Next, think of situations in which your team has made effective decisions and ineffective decisions. List those decisions.

Step 3

Classify the list of decisions according to the four categories on the matrix on page 141:

1. Leader handles these decisions; team members involved for learning.

2. Leader and team members collaborate on these decisions.

3. Leader coaches team members on these decisions; teams eventually take responsibility for them.

4. Teams make the decisions; leader stays in the background.

This matrix will help everyone see which decisions the teams can take responsibility for and which ones you and the teams can work on together.

Leader handles these decisions; team members involved for learning. **1**	Leader and team members collaborate on these decisions. **2**
Leader coaches team members on these decisions; teams eventually take responsibility for them. **3**	Teams make the decisions; leader stays in the background. **4**

HI

R i s k

LO

LO   **HI**

Team Experience

Step 4

Agree on how you will handle the decisions in each quadrant. Ask the team to discuss these questions.

1. How can the leader provide better coaching on the decisions in quadrant 3?

2. What can the team do to increase the leader's comfort in quadrant 4?

3. How would the team like to be involved in the tough decisions in quadrant 1?

4. How can the leader and team members collaborate in quadrant 2?

Notes. . .

Month 5

When to Call for Help

- You want to give the teams more challenging decisions but feel that others (such as purchasing, warehouse, lab) need to be involved first. Plan a meeting with the manager of the related department to discuss roles.

- Your team is experiencing a double dip in production and quality, according to your business plan's tracking systems. Ask your accounting group or your manager if the dip is a significant concern. Most likely the dip is temporary.

If You Do Nothing Else . . .

1. Assess your teams' self-directedness by rating their progress against the original Empowerment Schedule.

2. Start helping your teams analyze and improve their relationships with other internal partners.

3. Reevaluate which decisions you should be making and which ones the teams should be making.

Month at a Glance

MONDAY	TUESDAY	WEDNESDAY	THURSDAY	FRIDAY	SATURDAY/ SUNDAY
Pass on any new information to teams —30 minutes			Assess how well the teams are becoming self-directed —2 hours		
	Team meeting —2 hours Discuss their degree of self-directedness	Discuss progress on the business plan —3 hours	Coach team members on new tasks —2 hours		
Coach team members on new tasks —2 hours	Analyze teams' relationships with other teams —2 hours		Let my manager know how we're progressing —1 hour	Host open house of our areas for other groups —1 hour	
	Team meeting —2 hours	Evaluate who makes decisions —2 hours	Reinforce team members' skills learned in training —30 minutes	Review my skills training materials —30 minutes	

Time Budget

	Goal	Actual
Team coaching	50%	
Project work	10%	
Administrative	30%	
Personal development	10%	

Key Lessons

_____

_____

_____

_____

_____

_____

Next Steps

_____

_____

_____

_____

_____

_____

New Team Month 6

Notes. . .

Month 6

What to Expect

Your crew—that is, your team members—may have been drifting in circles for a little while. Be persistent in your effort to pull them on course. In the meantime, you can capitalize on the progress you have made. In fact, this month you can expect to see:

- Further evidence of behavior change in yourself and your team members.

- Team members working more efficiently on the tasks you've handed off to them.

- The ongoing need to give your teams opportunities to make more challenging decisions.

If your teams are already getting on course, you may be able to expand your own role by taking on a few challenging and fun tasks. Don't forget to spend time on projects that will fulfill you *and* assist your teams.

Possible Concerns

My area was redesigned. For the past six months we've been working in three teams. Our management would like me to help create more teams. I've heard what people are saying, and they're not buying all this change. I'd like to help, but is this my responsibility?

This problem is real and needs to be handled soon. Your job is to work with your senior management to provide the encouragement, incentives, and skills that will attract people to the teams. At one consumer products plant, management gave employees and leaders ample time to adjust to a team-based environment. Management announced that everyone would have two years to decide whether or not to join teams. Each employee would receive the skills required to be successful in a team environment. Any employees who wouldn't or couldn't join a team after the two-year training-decision period would be given an opportunity to work in one of the company's traditional plants.

Your Focus This Month

At this point in the teams' development, you will have a good opportunity to:

- Assess and tackle the most common barriers to team advancement.

- Reevaluate your role and how it's changing.

- Recognize six months of hard work.

Week 1
Common barriers and how to bust them

Reading the Barrier Barometer

Your teams probably are having some difficulty making decisions, planning projects, or taking on new responsibilities. Sometimes they're stymied by a lack of resources. Other times they face bigger obstacles to their progress. Your teams need your help if they're going to overcome these barriers. You can help by becoming a "boundary manager," tackling the external barriers so the teams can focus on their shared leadership tasks.

To navigate successfully around barriers, your teams need you to help pilot the ship. You can provide that help by first working with your teams to assess which barriers are the most difficult to navigate. Complete the "Barrier Barometer" with your teams. It will help you and them focus on the most dangerous barriers to team progress.

1. Circle the number that describes your teams' situation. Answer the "Acid Test" question to plot your spot on the continuum.

2. Complete the scoring form on page 148.

Barrier Barometer

1. Support groups' support

1	2	3	4	5

Our support groups hoard information and protect their turf.

Our support groups make the effort to share and explain the information we need.

Acid Test: If your team was trying to do a budget, would your accounting department willingly give them team-based cost data?

2. Acceptance by other managers

1	2	3	4	5

Other managers refuse to meet with team members or don't take them seriously.

Other managers accept meetings with team members as openly as they did with the supervisor.

Acid Test: Can a team member serve on a new vendor certification task force in your place?

3. Management support

1	2	3	4	5

Most managers only give the teams lip service; they are out of touch with team needs.

Our managers willingly turn decisions over to the teams and seriously consider team proposals.

Acid Test: If your team prepared a cross-training proposal that required additional overtime, would your manager approve it?

4. Incompatible systems

1	2	3	4	5

Our information, feedback, and compensation systems, or our layout, hamper our ability to work with other departments or customers.

Our information, feedback, and compensation systems, or our layout, enable us to work well with other departments and customers.

Acid Test: Do walls or noise prevent you from discussing problems with your internal customers or suppliers?

5. Conflicts with other teams

1	2	3	4	5

Other teams hamper our progress by taking resources we need or refusing to help us when the work load is heavy.

Other teams share our goals and collaborate with us on problems; they volunteer to help us when the work load is heavy.

Acid Test: If your organization could afford to buy only one piece of equipment, could you count on the other teams you work with to share it?

Continued on next page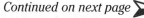

Barometer Scoring

Review the five barrier categories. A rating of 4 or 5 means that this barrier is not a problem now. A rating of 3 or less means you and your teams have a barrier that needs to be addressed. (Remember: Even positive positions have a way of growing weak in time. You and your teams need to be vigilant to make sure a strength today doesn't become a weakness tomorrow.)

Write your teams' top two barriers in the spaces provided. An example is provided in italics. With them, develop some ways to prevent the barrier from slowing down the teams' progress or to minimize its impact on the teams. Write your ideas in the spaces provided.

Top Two Barriers	
Sample barrier: *Support group support*	Specifically, the barrier here is: *The team would like to order some of its own supplies. The supply department is a bottleneck, and we need supplies more quickly.*
Barrier #1:	Specifically, the barrier here is:
Barrier #2:	Specifically, the barrier here is:

Week 2
More on busting barriers

Review the five barriers you assessed last week. Focus on those barriers that you and the teams identified as the ones you want to work on first. With the teams, agree on the actions everyone can take to prevent, overcome, bypass, or minimize the barriers. Write your ideas for responding to team barriers in the spaces provided.

Resistant Support Groups (such as accounting, lab, maintenance, human resources, engineering)

Possible Causes

- Lack of understanding about the team concept.

- Unclear roles/responsibilities.

- Conflicting goals or priorities.

How to Respond

- ☐ Educate support groups about the benefits and implications of teams.

- ☐ Go through the team start-up process with the problem support group to clarify goals, roles, and responsibilities.

- ☐ Invite support group members to team meetings to build understanding and rapport.

Your Ideas

Rejection by Other Managers

Possible Causes

- Lack of understanding of team members' expertise and capabilities.

- Long-standing comfort with the chain of command.

How to Respond

- ☐ Have your team members demonstrate their expertise with their new responsibilities. Pave the way by telling other managers that you have confidence in your team members' abilities and expertise.

- ☐ Ask other managers to describe their ideas for solving this problem.

Your Ideas

Lack of Management Support

Possible Causes

- No time to spend on learning about teams.

- Vague or conflicting direction from top management.

- Don't see this as a priority.

- Bound to tradition.

How to Respond

- ☐ Educate your high-level champions. Get them interested in your progress.

- ☐ Link the implementation of empowered teams to achieving specific business goals.

- ☐ Ask each manager to sign an agreement stating what he or she will do to support empowered teams.

Your Ideas

Incompatible Systems (such as compensation, information systems, performance management, facility layout, budgets)

Possible Causes

- Systems are changing and the new processes are not fully understood yet.

- Managers don't understand the need to change systems for teams.

How to Respond

- ☐ Discuss with managers how systems are slowing down your teams' progress.

- ☐ Prepare a proposal for a small, specific system change.

- ☐ Ask support professionals to attend a team meeting to explain system change options.

Your Ideas

Conflicts with Other Teams

Possible Causes

- Scarce resources.

- Pressure to outperform each other.

- Infrequent meetings.

How to Respond

- ☐ Brainstorm a schedule for sharing equipment or tasks.

- ☐ Plan a joint celebration event.

- ☐ Schedule monthly problem-solving meetings with all the members of both teams.

- ☐ Review common goals in both teams' charters.

Your Ideas

Week 3
Did I spend my time wisely?

How Has Your Job Changed?

You, the leader, are key to making empowered teams happen in your organization. Teams cannot become empowered until your role changes. In addition, the more you work at changing your role, the greater your chance to take on more interesting work.

Complete the three parts of this assessment to get a picture of your changing role and what you can do to become even more effective.

Part 1

Refer to the role definition on page 46. Fill in the blanks at right to compare the percent of time you spent on each activity three months ago and how you spend your time now. The sample shows the change for one leader.

Sample

	Then	Now
Personal Development	2%	15%
Administrative/Paperwork	25%	15%
Special Projects	5%	10%
Coaching	15%	45%
Day-to-day Coordination	53%	15%

	Then	Now
Personal Development	____%	____%
Administrative/Paperwork	____%	____%
Special Projects	____%	____%
Coaching	____%	____%
Day-to-day Coordination	____%	____%

Part 2

Use the following guidelines to gauge your progress against that of successful team leaders:

- The amount of time you spend in day-to-day coordination should be smaller now (for most leaders, this is reduced by half at the six-month mark).

- You should be spending about twice as much time coaching (transferring tasks and developing star points).

- The time you spend on paperwork should have dropped by at least one-third.

- Your personal development will remain the same as you pick up more responsibility yourself.

Part 3

In which areas are you on target, and in which are you below target? Write your answers in the space provided. Then read the tips for how you can improve areas that are weak. Add your own ideas to the list of improvement tips.

Areas that are on target:

Areas where my role is below target or expectations:

If you're having trouble with:	Try:
• Coaching	• Scheduling coaching appointments with team members. • Keeping a coaching list on your desk or in your computer of who to coach on what.
• Personal Development	• Planning or scheduling training and development dates on your calendar. • Asking your manager to hold you accountable for specific goals and activities in the area of personal development.
• Administrative Paperwork	• Working with other supervisors to eliminate paperwork. • Automating some functions.
• Day-to-day Coordination	• Asking team members what day-to-day tasks you still might be too involved in.

Week 4
Recognizing six months of hard work

You and your teams have come a long way! Congratulations! You are halfway through the New Team Phase of team development. Take time out to reflect on your progress. Show the team the forest as opposed to the trees by helping them recall progress during the last six months.

Share War Stories

Think of some interesting stories with your team that describe where you were six months ago in terms of:

- Attitudes *(For example, "Remember when we all thought the team concept was a pipe dream? Now we really see the benefits. . . .")*

- Behaviors *(For example, "I remember when I said I would never cross-train with sales. Now I perform several sales functions, and it makes life easier for me, sales, and the customer!")*

- Output *(For example, "We were good performers before teams. But now that we have changed the work process, we are getting results our equipment suppliers didn't think were even possible.")*

- Quality *(For example, "Before teams, quality was checked randomly—and way down the line. Now everyone takes responsibility for quality. There's been a big improvement in quality, and everyone can feel good about it.")*

- Service *(For example, "Before we all were cross-trained, if customers called with questions I couldn't answer, I'd pass them on to an expert. It was frustrating for me, but I can just imagine how the client felt getting shuttled around.")*

A Pat on the Back

What are some of your teams' biggest accomplishments in terms of:

- Attitudes?

- Behaviors?

- Output?

- Quality?

- Service?

Proud Because . . .

What are you most proud of as a team? During a team meeting ask each team member to describe the one event, thing, action, or achievement he or she is most proud of. Ask the team, "What achievement do we single out as our best?"

For example:

☐ Attracting new customers.

☐ Earning repeat business.

☐ Gaining flexibility; responding to changes more quickly.

☐ Getting along without knocking each other down.

☐ Solving shift-change problems.

Looking Ahead

Discuss where the team is going in the future, what you can expect to celebrate in the future, and what the team can look forward to the most in the future.

Notes. . .

Month 6

When to Call for Help

- If you cannot get the resources you need to overcome barriers. Watch out! This type of issue can sink your teams (or stall them, at the very least). Keep pushing to get the resources you need.

- You can't seem to give the teams the coaching time they need (50 percent) because of competing demands. If you can't meet your coaching time budget, discuss it with your manager—don't wait until it's too late.

If You Do Nothing Else . . .

1. Objectively analyze the barriers your team is bumping into and plan corrective action.

2. Take a break and pat yourself on the back for all that you and your teams have done.

3. Thank support group members who have contributed to your progress.

Month at a Glance

MONDAY	TUESDAY	WEDNESDAY	THURSDAY	FRIDAY	SATURDAY/ SUNDAY
Update the teams —30 minutes	Team meeting —2 hours Complete Barrier Barometer; prioritize barriers with teams		Let the team know how my meeting with our manager went —1 hour		
	With the team, develop tactics to address our top barriers —2 hours			Follow up on performance problems—how is it going? —1 hour	
Coaching discussion for me with a black belt leader —2 hours			Assess how my role has changed —1 hour	Plan actions to make sure I'm on track with my role —1 hour	
	Six-month milestone celebration —3 hours		Leader skills training —4 hours		

Time Budget

	Goal	Actual
Team coaching	50%	
Project work	10%	
Administrative	30%	
Personal development	10%	

Key Lessons

_____
_____
_____
_____
_____
_____

Next Steps

_____
_____
_____
_____
_____
_____

Notes...

Notes....

New Team Maintenance Phase

Congratulations! By now you and your new teams should be sailing on an even keel. During the next six months your teams will not only discover the secrets to maintaining momentum, they'll also chart new territory. Use the activities on the following pages to guide you through the New Team Maintenance Phase.

Month 7

- Team leader sanity check
- Are your teams ready for more responsibility?
- Secrets to transferring responsibilities
- The changing nature of team meetings

Month 8

- Connecting teams with internal suppliers
- Refocusing on the vision and values
- Check out those results!
- Three cheers for us!

Month 9

- Analyzing team meetings
- Making team training stick
- Your role as a boundary manager: Customer advocate
- Getting out of meetings

Month 10

- Checkpoint #5: What's your next move?
- Life after coaching: Advancing your role
- Oops!—When a team makes a major mistake
- Learning from other leaders

Month 11

- Asking for feedback from the teams
- Helping your teams make better decisions
- Providing tailor-made coaching
- Encouraging team initiative

Month 12

- Taking the teams' temperature—Part 2
- Developing a broader business perspective
- Renewing the teams
- Celebrating progress

New Team Month 7

Notes. . .

What to Expect

It's been seven months since your teams were formed. Now you can expect them to be coming out of that phase in which they floated in circles. With the proper training and support, they should be Getting on Course.

4. Full Speed Ahead

1. Getting Started

2. Going in Circles

3. Getting on Course

You may notice that the team seems to get to the point more directly in meetings and that they are more willing to solve problems than bicker over them. This is a gradual process, so don't be disappointed if you see some backsliding.

Overall, you should be seeing the following trends:

- Constructive problem solving

- Acknowledgement and acceptance of differences in styles, perspectives, and approaches to problems

- Fewer emotional outbursts

Possible Concerns

Help! Instead of subsiding, the conflict in our group seems to be getting worse. Last week a fistfight almost broke out in a team meeting!

The operative phrase here is "seems to be getting worse." Problems and conflict in the group probably always existed. Team members just weren't willing to acknowledge it.

Many teams go through a stage full of bickering, complaining, blaming, and accusing. Look on the bright side: This could be a sign that the teams are coming to grips with their problems rather than ignoring or burying them.

Your job is to help them deal with these problems in a more constructive manner. Other team leaders have found the following techniques helpful:

- Reinforce that this phase is natural and all teams go through it.

- Provide refresher training and coaching in handling conflict and valuing differences.

- Use conflict management techniques when facilitating the group: help them identify the superordinate goal; get them to focus on the problem, not the person, etc.

- Reconsider the group's operating guidelines to see if you need to include rules for dealing with conflict.

Your Focus This Month

Maintaining the teams' growth this month will find you:

- Checking your own sanity.

- Gauging how much responsibility your teams can take on.

- Learning new ways of passing on responsibilities to teams.

- Looking at the changing nature of team meetings.

Week 1
Team leader sanity check

Sometimes leaders of new teams feel as if they're "losing it." These feelings often peak after the six-month mark, so now is a good time to check your sanity. See where you fit in below:

Normal

- ☐ Your teams are alternately frustrating and rewarding.

- ☐ You have occasional setbacks and make mistakes.

- ☐ Even when you ask for advice, your manager doesn't always seem to know what to do.

Over-the-edge

- ☐ Your relationship with the teams is so bad you've considered applying for the witness protection program.

- ☐ You feel that the last time you did something right was in the Eisenhower administration.

- ☐ You've given up talking to your manager altogether.

Laboratory studies show that rats and guinea pigs go crazy when they are put in a maze and punished for things over which they have no control. This principle also applies to team leaders. That is why (if you want to outperform the rats) you need to analyze the causes of your frustration and take action.

Take time out now to identify what drives you crazy about leading teams:

1.

2.

3.

If you're having trouble coming up with something, consider the following common causes of frustration among new team leaders.

Cause #1

"The team rejects my advice/coaching."

How to remain sane:

- Discuss the issue with the team.

- Examine your own behavior; ask the team what you can do to provide more help.

- Agree on required outcomes with the team; let the team approach the task in their own way as long as they achieve the agreed-on outcomes.

Cause #2

"Management says they want teams, but they don't let me make decisions or mistakes."

How to remain sane:

- Negotiate more autonomy with your manager; ask for more latitude in making several specific decisions.

- Show you've learned from mistakes by devising processes that keep them from recurring.

Cause #3

"Teams want more responsibility than they are ready for."

How to remain sane:

- Allow them to handle new responsibilities with your coaching; then pull back when they have demonstrated that they can handle each new task.

Cause #4

"I'm not good at leading teams."

How to remain sane:

- Don't give up yet. Many team leaders find that it takes six to twelve months to feel competent.

- Ask for feedback on how you're doing from your manager and your teams.

- Attend refresher training.

Cause #5

"Leading teams is so time consuming."

How to remain sane:

- There is an awkward period when it takes you longer to coach the team to do something than it would to do it yourself. This investment in coaching and training should pay off within the next few months.

- In the meantime, you may want to renegotiate a few tasks with your manager. Some (such as routine meetings) can be dropped temporarily; others (such as discretionary projects) can be postponed.

Do not despair! Things will get better. Teams will become more competent, and the organization will become more supportive as the team effort matures. List at least two specific actions that will address your frustrations:

Week 2
Are your teams ready for more responsibility?

Reality Check

Team members may not always recognize when they're ready for more challenging assignments. However, if they're lined up at your door begging for more responsibility, you've waited too long to turn over some of your tasks and duties to them.

Use the following checklist to determine whether it's time for you to consider transferring more tasks or decisions to the team. Read each item and put a check mark in the box if that situation applies to you.

☐ At least 60 percent of the team members can successfully handle their current tasks.

☐ Team members have time to complain about other teams, bicker among themselves, and generally act out their dissatisfaction on the job.

☐ It's been more than two months since the team learned anything new.

☐ Other teams, started at about the same time, are doing more than your teams.

☐ Team members aren't as excited about or absorbed in what they're doing as they used to be.

If you checked two or more of the boxes above, it's time to act now!

What to Transfer

Completing the three parts of this section will give you a better idea of what to pass on and how willing and ready you are to do that.

Part 1

What I do now (that I might not have to do)

1. List two things you do each week that have become routine:

   (1)

   (2)

2. What meetings do you attend that a team member could attend instead?

3. What reports do you complete that a team member could do instead?

Part 2

Are you ready to let go?

Often the team is ready for new challenges before the leader is ready to let go. Evaluate your own feelings about the status quo by checking those statements that apply to you:

☐ I like doing everything I do now.

☐ I don't think the team will do it as well as me.

☐ If the team makes a mistake, I'm afraid it will reflect badly on me.

☐ I don't have time to really show them how to do the task.

☐ I don't think the team would be interested in trying something new.

☐ It's really my responsibility to do these things.

If you checked more than one item above, you might be an obstacle to the teams.

Part 3

Services, tasks, or decisions that support departments currently handle

Identify three support departments or teams with which your teams routinely interact. What tasks or decisions do those departments or teams currently handle for your teams?

Support departments	Task/Decisions they currently handle for the team
Human resources	*Interview candidates for opening on the team (could be done by the team).*

A. Pick a task from Part 1 or Part 3 that you could transfer to the team:

B. Who on your teams is ready to take on the task? (You can identify more than one person.)

C. Identify three things you need to do to transfer the task (training, information, support, etc.):

Week 3
Secrets to transferring responsibilities

When your teams are clamoring for more responsibility, you need to respond quickly. But, you ask, how? This week you'll review some ideas on how to give your teams responsibility.

Most team responsibilities fall into one of two categories:

Category 1: Tasks everyone on the team must do simultaneously. For example:

- New housekeeping tasks

- Learning and using e-mail

- Complying with safety regulations

- New quality tracking responsibilities

Category 2: Tasks that are best performed by one member (such as a coordinator or star point) on behalf of the team. For example:

- Attending the quality meeting

- Reporting the team's daily results

- Running team meetings

1. **Determine in which category your task falls.**

   Doing so will dictate whether you are training one person or an entire team.

2. **Explain to the teams why the task is important and why it's being turned over to them.**

   Discuss the benefits to the organization and to the teams. Benefits to the team might include: more immediate feedback, the ability to control variances in their work, or being able to operate more like their own business.

3. **Explain the support that will be available.**

   Support typically includes training, ongoing coaching, or follow-up from an expert and some way for them to monitor their progress on the task.

4. **Agree with teams on how you and they will know that the task is being performed effectively.**

   These agreements constitute the criteria for successfully transferring the task—the point

at which the teams officially own the new responsibility. Be sure to specify only your minimum conditions for success so the teams have some freedom to decide how to do the task.

5. **Establish a follow-up plan with the teams.**

   It helps to establish several follow-up dates with the teams so you can be sure they are getting all the help they need to perform the new tasks effectively. Be sure the teams understand that follow-up meetings are to provide support, not to "check up on them."

One Leader's Transfer Plan

Following is a plan developed by one leader for turning over more responsibilities to his teams:

1. Teams must start tracking their expenses against budget. Everyone will enter expenses on computer log; one member will compile monthly expense reports.

2. This is an important responsibility because next year's team compensation will be based partly on expense control. The teams need to get the hang of expense management now, and tracking their expenses gives them immediate feedback.

3. Everyone will receive two hours of training in accessing the expense log on the computer. The administrative coordinator will receive an additional five hours of training in analyzing monthly expense reports. For two months I'll continue the manual tracking system as a backup. Pat from accounting has offered to come to the next team meeting to discuss ideas for controlling expenses.

4. We'll know it's working when all expenses are properly coded and the team is operating within budget six months in a row.

5. I'll meet one-on-one with each team member in the week after training. We'll review expense performance as a team once a month, starting on the 20th.

Your Transfer Plan

Answer the following questions to create your own responsibility transfer plan:

1. Is this a task that:

    a. Everyone on the team must do?

    b. Is best performed by one member on behalf of the team? Who?

2. Why is the task important, and why is it being turned over to the team?

3. What support will be available?

4. How will I and the team know that the task is being performed effectively?

5. Follow-up date(s):

Week 4
The changing nature of team meetings

As your teams mature, they will become increasingly sophisticated about what they discuss in team meetings. At first, teams are comfortable discussing mostly technical information. Then they reach the point where they discuss team and interpersonal problems. As fully mature teams, they will not only focus on business issues, but they'll spend more of their time actually solving problems rather than just reporting information.

The chart at right illustrates how one team spent its time during a team meeting. This interaction pattern is typical of teams in this stage of development.

Sample Time Form

		Type of information discussed		
		Technical	**Team/Interpersonal**	**Business**
How it was handled by the team	**Reporting Information** (little or no problem solving or decision making)	• *The pump on line 3 is down. (10 minutes of discussion)* • *12 minutes explaining the new preventive maintenance schedule*	• *Anne is late to the meeting again. (8 minutes of complaining about Anne's behavior)*	• *2 minutes reporting on a change in sales trends*
	Solving/Deciding Issues (action items result from the discussion)	• *15 minutes used to figure out how to prevent line downtime*		

What Are Your Teams Doing?

Attend a meeting of one of your teams. Use the form on this page to chart their interaction patterns.

Review how the team spent its time. Do the following if:

- Your team spends too much time reporting information rather than solving problems.

  Occasionally lengthen the time for team meetings. It's hard to solve problems in 15 to 30 minutes.

- The team spends too little time on team or interpersonal problems.

  Interview team members before the meeting. Find out what team or interpersonal problems might be going unaddressed. Coach one of the team members to raise the issue.

- The team is not spending enough time discussing business issues.

  Make reporting on key business indicators a standing agenda item.

  Arrange for customers or business experts to attend the meetings to raise awareness about business concerns.

		Type of information discussed		
		Technical	**Team/Interpersonal**	**Business**
How it was handled by the team	**Reporting Information**			
	Solving/Deciding Issues			

Notes. . .

Month 7

When to Call for Help

- You may need to get an outside perspective if you and your team can't agree on how much responsibility they can handle. If you suspect that neither you nor the team is viewing the situation objectively, ask a third party (trainer, facilitator, your manager) to coach you through the activities in Week 2.

- If as a result of the "sanity check" you figure you are really over the edge, it would probably help to get advice from other leaders of teams.

If You Do Nothing Else . . .

1. Evaluate your teams' readiness for more responsibility.

2. Assess your own willingness to let go.

3. Transfer at least one new responsibility to the teams.

Month at a Glance

MONDAY	TUESDAY	WEDNESDAY	THURSDAY	FRIDAY	SATURDAY/ SUNDAY
Do a sanity check —1 hour					
	Identify three responsibilities to transfer —1 hour		Meet with manager and check progress —1 hour		
Turn over first responsibility —1 hour	Provide coaching on new responsibility —1 hour		Turn over second responsibility —1 hour	Provide coaching on second responsibility —1 hour	
Analyze team meeting and give feedback to the team —2 hours		Turn over third responsibility —1 hour	Provide coaching on third responsibility —1 hour		

Time Budget

	Goal	Actual
Team coaching	60%	
Project work	10%	
Administrative	15%	
Personal development	15%	

Key Lessons

_____

_____

_____

_____

_____

_____

Next Steps

_____

_____

_____

_____

_____

_____

New Team Month 8

Notes. . .

Month

8

What to Expect

At last, your teams should be starting to hit a steady stride. At least they're all in the same boat, and they've stopped hitting each other over the head with the paddles! They may even have the paddles in the water and be rowing in the same direction.

Possible Concerns

Is it possible for teams to be "too full of themselves?" Suddenly my team doesn't want to have anything to do with anyone else. They think they can do it all themselves, and they're rejecting all help. They've adopted a sort of competitive attitude toward other teams: not sharing information and plotting to beat other teams.

This response is not only possible, it's fairly common. But it's appropriate for you to be concerned, too. Many leaders are so relieved that their teams have started to become more cohesive, they don't care that they have banded together against outsiders. Unfortunately, if this attitude persists, the team runs the risk of developing a reputation for being elitist.

This month contains some suggestions on how to break down barriers between your teams and other internal groups. Later sections will provide advice on developing better relationships between your teams and their customers.

Now that my teams seem to have hit some kind of steady state (at least their team processes and procedures are under control), they don't want to meet as often as before. (We had been meeting for a 10-minute update in the morning and for one hour once a week.)

You should never force a team to meet if there is no legitimate business reason for the meeting. Meetings are expensive; you should evaluate their return on investment as with any business activity.

This does not mean that you should give up on your one-hour weekly meetings. Team members might be reluctant to go to those meetings because they don't think they're getting anything new or helpful out of them. Ask for their feedback and consider doing the following:

- If they have been discussing team procedures, try getting them to identify a persistent team or technical problem they can work on.

- If they've been working on problems within the team or the unit, try coaching them to identify problems with suppliers or customers.

Your Focus This Month

This month your focus will be on:

- Helping the teams build stronger relationships with their internal suppliers.

- Refocusing on the vision and values.

- Checking results against your baseline.

- Celebrating success.

Week 1
Connecting teams with internal suppliers

Your teams might be ready to think outside their own boundaries. They will do this successfully only with your assistance; it's your job to help them build better relationships with their internal partners. Strong relationships are the links to better performance.

Often internal suppliers are the source of much complaining and misunderstanding. It's common for a team to blame its internal partners for all kinds of failings, mistakes, snafus, and delays. When a team has had trouble producing a product or delivering a service, team members often are quick to point the finger of blame at some other department or unit and say, "If only (insert department or team) would (insert complaint), we could do our jobs better!"

One Approach

Complete the following two-step exercise to help your teams attack this situation head on.

Step 1

Working with your teams, identify up to four groups that supply the teams with information, products, or services.

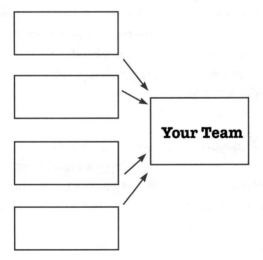

Purchasing vs. Mail Room

Many of the problems with internal suppliers stem from misunderstandings about needs and requirements. This was the case at one organization where a feud developed between the purchasing group and the mail room team. Purchasing team members believed that the mail room crew deliberately delayed their packages. Mail room team members believed that purchasing willfully disregarded coding procedures in their perpetual last-minute rush to get things done.

Step 2

Have your teams meet with one of their internal suppliers. (If not everyone can attend such a meeting, arrange for representatives from both groups to get together.) Help the two groups establish a joint goal. Discuss each group's needs and identify what the two groups have to do to meet each other's needs and achieve the joint goal. Before the meeting, coach your team members on nonconfrontational meeting behaviors; but be prepared to mediate any conflicts that arise.

Ask the two teams to complete a form similar to the one at right. The example contains information discussed and agreed to by the purchasing and mail room groups in the situation cited above.

Sample Agreement Form

Joint Goal	Purchasing's Needs	Mail Room's Needs	Agreements
Getting mail out on time.	*Need requests for bids to be sent out same day.*	*Need an account code on each overnight delivery package.*	• *Purchasing will supply the mail room with standard account codes.* • *New projects will be sent down with new codes.* • *Overnight packages will go out the same day.* • *If there are any problems or questions, Mike and Tina will call each other.*

Week 2
Refocusing on the vision and values

It's easy to lose sight of the original direction as the teams get caught up in the day-to-day challenges of managing their business. It's your role as a leader periodically to get out the map and refocus everybody on where you and they are headed.

Revisiting the Vision

Review your vision; what has worked that you might want to try again?

What didn't work that you might want to avoid in the future?

Consider these ideas for refocusing your teams on the vision:

- Set aside time in a team meeting to analyze how well the group is living the vision and values.

- Ask the top leader at your site to discuss the vision and values with the team during a team meeting.

- Ask the team to evaluate you on how well you're modeling and supporting the vision and values.

Living the Values

Your behavior plays a key role in shaping your team members' attitudes about the values. Most effective team leaders have found ways that they can reinforce the values. Consider the following examples:

Values	Leader's Acts
Hospital value of high-touch patient care	*A staff development leader goes to work one hour early once a week so she can talk with patients about what's important to them about their care. They discuss the care they receive, the hospital personnel they interact with, their rooms, and housekeeping performance.*
Manufacturing plant value of open communication	*The commercial products leader holds a "discuss-the-undiscussables" meeting once a quarter. At this meeting team members can ask about and discuss issues that historically have been unmentionable (for instance, what will happen when the plant manager retires).*

List your organization's values in the left column. For each value, identify one action you can take as a leader to reinforce and demonstrate your commitment to that value. Refer to best practice statements in the Preteam Phase (see page 11) as a reminder.

Organizational Values	Action You Can Take

Week 3
Check out those results!

Your teams have been monitoring their performance for some time. Now is a good time to help the teams interpret the data. Look for trends or gaps in performance. Following are some typical irregularities or trends in performance and suggestions for how to address them.

Goal Overshoot

Goal overshoot usually is represented by a sudden, sharp jump beyond the stated goal. This might be due to factors beyond your control (a drop in price, an increase in orders), or it might indicate a success factor you can exploit (supplier delivered raw materials early).

What you should do:

1. With your teams, analyze the cause.

2. Determine if there is anything you or the teams can do to get the cause to happen regularly.

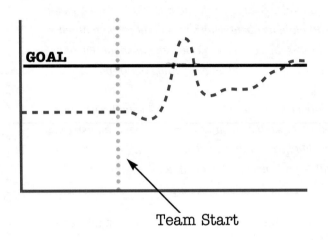

Team Start

Initial Learning Time

Efficiency might decrease when people are learning a new procedure or starting to work together as a team. This drop in efficiency might continue until everyone feels more comfortable with the technical and team processes.

What you should do:

1. Reassure the teams that this drop in efficiency is normal.

2. Check to make sure the team members are receiving all the training and support they need.

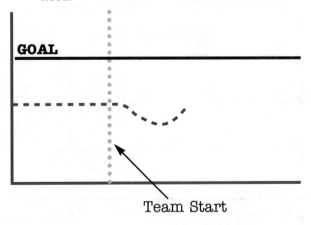

Team Start

Approaching Goal

Sometimes your teams will come very close to reaching a goal but not quite get there. This could indicate that the goal has been set too high or that your own reinforcement, encouragement, and focus have tapered off.

What you should do:

1. Refocus on the goal and review its importance with the teams.

2. Help the teams brainstorm ways to close the gap between performance and goal achievement.

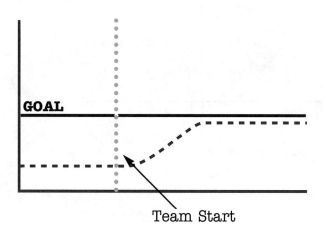

Goal Attainment and Falloff

Your teams might be achieving their goals consistently, then for some reason, start falling short of the goals. This might indicate that the teams have let some of the old, inefficient procedures creep back into the picture. You can prevent this from happening by continuing to monitor team performance after the goal has been attained.

What you should do:

1. Analyze the causes for the falloff with the team.

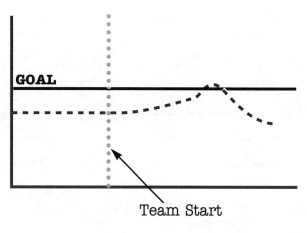

No Effect

The chart of your teams' progress might indicate that there has been little or no effect on the factor you are measuring. This could mean that more than one factor is affecting your performance. At this point it's best to consult with your manager or other outside experts.

Week 4

Your teams have come a long way. So now you should consider holding another formal celebration to mark the teams' accomplishments. It's your responsibility to create some hoopla for the team and help them get recognition for the progress they've made. First you will want to determine what to celebrate, then decide how to celebrate.

What to Celebrate

By this point in their evolution, the teams should be able to point to some technical improvements or improved business results. This chart allows you to note those accomplishments. The left column contains ideas for the kinds of things your teams can celebrate. Review the examples of team accomplishments, then write your teams' accomplishments in the space provided.

Celebrate	Examples	Team Accomplishments
Team business results • Achieving a goal • Hitting a milestone that will enable you to reach a goal (progress against baseline) • Improving some indicator over last year's performance	• *Hitting service delivery goals three months in a row* • *15 percent ahead of first quarter's projections* • *25 percent improvement in first-time yield over last year*	
External recognition • Positive feedback from a customer • Team mentioned in company newsletter	• *Letter from top customer pledging more business* • *Team's completion of training recognized*	
Technical improvements • Completing a problem-solving project • Getting approval to implement a team's suggested process improvement	• *Scanner downtime solution approved* • *Purchase of new press approved*	

How to Celebrate

Keep the following guidelines in mind when planning team celebrations:

- The reason for the recognition should be clearly stated and understood. Do not throw a party for its own sake.

- The celebration should not antagonize other teams. Avoid celebrating that your teams have "beat" other teams.

There are a number of ways to celebrate technical accomplishments, some of which you've probably tried already.

- Submit a news release about the team's accomplishment to your local newspaper.

- Send a personal note to each team member at home.

- Arrange for the top leader to treat the team to lunch.

- Arrange for the team to present its accomplishments at a management meeting.

- Erect a big sign in a prominent location describing the team's accomplishment.

Because you'll want your teams to celebrate their own accomplishments, involve one or more members in planning the celebration. Ask the person or persons chosen for this job to help complete the chart below.

Team Accomplishments (from page 180)	How to Celebrate	When to Celebrate

Notes. . .

When to Call for Help

- If other internal partners are not receptive to the overtures you or your teams make, you may need to get outside help to bring the groups together. If appeals to the other teams' leaders haven't worked, facilitators from the training or human resources department often can help bring groups together.

- If you sense that your team is tired of hearing about the vision from you, it may be more energizing to bring in an outside speaker (such as the site manager or the sales director) to help the team refocus on the vision.

If You Do Nothing Else . . .

1. Refocus on the vision and values (checking your own behavior as well as the teams' progress).

2. Evaluate the teams' results against the original baseline measures you established.

3. Celebrate progress—toward the vision or against the baseline.

Month at a Glance

MONDAY	TUESDAY	WEDNESDAY	THURSDAY	FRIDAY	SATURDAY/ SUNDAY
Analyze relationship with other areas —2 hours	Follow up with team on new responsibilities; provide coaching —1 hour		Work side-by-side with team; provide coaching —8 hours		
	Refocus team on vision —2 hours		Examine own use of values —1 hour		
		Check results against baseline —2 hours		Progress check with manager —1 hour	
Mini Team Celebration —15 minutes		Coach team to implement solution to improve relations with one internal partner —2 hours			

Time Budget

	Goal	Actual
Team coaching	60%	
Project work	10%	
Administrative	15%	
Personal development	15%	

Key Lessons

_____

_____

_____

_____

_____

_____

Next Steps

_____

_____

_____

_____

_____

_____

New Team Month 9

Notes. . .

Month 9

What to Expect

Your teams should be very comfortable with the technical aspects of their work by now. All your team members should have a good understanding of each other's jobs, and they should be making significant progress on their cross-training plan.

These developments have important implications for you as a leader:

1. You should be free from the demands of day-to-day technical problem solving and coaching.

2. With a strong technical foundation, your teams should be ready to take on increasingly sophisticated process improvement projects and to concentrate on team business issues.

Your challenge is to avoid complacency—to continue to develop yourself and the teams. Leaders who allow themselves and the teams to rest on their technical laurels never experience the full benefits of high-performance teams.

Possible Concerns

I can't be sure, but I think one of my teams has run out of steam. They don't seem to be improving as rapidly as they were in the first few months. No one's complaining yet, but I'm worried that this may be the beginning of the end.

Your concern for your team shows that you're sensitive to issues dealing with progress and advancement. Signs of a team stalling, some of which you might have witnessed, include:

- A lack of excitement about working in teams.

- No one has learned anything new in the last couple of months.

- Business improvements have stopped. (Don't be alarmed if improvements are achieved at a slower rate; that is perfectly normal for developing teams. By this time many teams have "picked the low-hanging fruit"—now they may be tracking more complex problems without a quick or obvious payoff.)

If any of these apply to your teams, consider re-energizing the teams by:

- Giving them new, challenging responsibilities.

- Celebrating their accomplishments.

- Removing barriers between the teams and top management or customers. (The increased contact will give team members an opportunity to get reinforcement from other sources.)

Your Focus This Month

This month gives you several opportunities to:

- Analyze the team meeting process.

- Reinforce team training.

- Help the teams focus on relationships with internal customers.

- Coach team members to attend meetings in your place.

Week 1
Analyzing team meetings

You can help your teams have productive meetings by offering to observe them in action. As a "process observer," you would:

1. Attend a team meeting as an observer, taking notes on meeting behavior.

2. Talk with meeting participants about your observations at the end of the meeting.

3. Help team members agree on specific actions they could take to continue to improve meeting performance.

To do all this effectively, you must:

- Get the team's buy-in to the "process observer" idea.

- Agree on the behaviors you should track with the team.

- Make it clear that you are reviewing the entire team's performance, not just the meeting leader's performance.

- After the meeting involve the team in evaluating its performance.

What to Look For

Review the following categories and questions. Discuss this list with the team before the meeting you observe and together agree on the areas you should focus on.

Content

- Did the team focus on the most important, not just the most urgent, issues?

- Did everyone have an opportunity to contribute to the agenda?

- Was at least 40 percent of the meeting spent making decisions or planning actions?

- Were any important issues or perspectives swept under the rug?

Process

- Was the purpose and importance of the meeting clear?

- Were relevant details and data brought out in the open?

- Did the team adequately explore alternatives?

- Was everyone included in the discussion?

- Did team members build on each other's ideas?

- Was everyone's self-esteem maintained?

- Did the team use agreed-upon techniques to analyze problems and identify solutions?

- Was the plan of action clear?

- Were team members' needs and styles considered in making assignments?

- Were follow-up procedures clear?

Meeting Traps

- Did the team spend more than five percent of the time wandering off the subject?

- Was there evidence that one member or one faction dominated the discussion?

- Was any member of the team withdrawn?

- Did the team unnecessarily rethink decisions it had already made?

- Were issues raised without coming to closure?

Using the check sheet below, insert those items from the list that you and the team members have agreed you will focus on in your observation. An example is provided.

Observation Check Sheet

Content	Yes	No	Improvement Actions
Did the team focus on the most important, not just the most urgent, issues?		✔	*Classify all agenda items by importance before beginning. Start with most important.*

Week 2
Making team training stick

The Situation

Your team members have received a great deal of technical, interpersonal, and team training by now. Over time their skills will fade unless you provide the support and reinforcement they need to keep their newly acquired knowledge finely honed. The investment you, the organization, and the individual team members have made in this training is significant: It's not uncommon for team members to have 40 hours of training under their belts by now. It's your job to ensure that 40 hours have not been wasted.

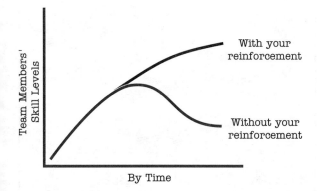

The Solution

The following chart contains some of the most common types of training programs. Check those that your teams have completed. Review the list of strategies (Leader Support Activities) you can take to further support your teams' training. Add your own ideas to this list. In the third column note who you will be working with (if applicable) and when you want to address the issue.

Team Training	Leader Support Activities	With Whom, By When
☐ **Participating in Meetings**	• Ask each team member to evaluate his or her own participation after each meeting. • Review the guidelines for participating before each meeting. • Post meeting guidelines in team meeting room.	
☐ **Leading Meetings**	• Ask each team member to take a turn leading a team meeting; provide coaching before and after. • Model the skills.	
☐ **Rescuing Difficult Meetings**	• Review the guidelines with the meeting leader before particularly difficult meetings.	

Team Training	Leader Support Activities	With Whom, By When
☐ **Reaching Agreement in Teams**	• Use at least one consensus tool in every meeting. • Post an impact/effort grid (or other decision-making chart) in your office.	
☐ **Valuing Differences**	• Review team members' interpersonal/decision-making styles at least once a quarter. • Guide the team to consider each others' styles when making assignments. • Refer to styles to explain and resolve conflicts.	

☐ **Interpersonal Skills**
 	
  • **Communicating with Others**
 	
  • **Supporting Others**
 	
  • **Handling Conflict**
	• When someone hears a team member use a key communication principle, put the member's name in a jar. Every month have a drawing for a prize.
	
	• Assign "buddies" within the team to provide coaching and reinforcement to each other.
	
	• Appoint a special conflict facilitator in each meeting to look for unresolved conflicts.	

☐ **Technical Skills**	• Arrange for team members to train new members in technical skills. • Ask team members to let you know when they are using the skill for the first time. Provide coaching and reinforcement. • Set up a large cross-training matrix in your team area; track everyone's progress. • Have the team nominate "master trainers" in each major technical skill area.	
☐ **Quality Skills**	• Encourage the formation of several problem-solving teams. • Use at least one quality tool in each meeting you conduct. • Whenever anyone presents a problem, ask for the root cause. • Set up a quality improvement board to showcase success stories.	

Week 3
Your role as boundary manager: Customer advocate

In New Team Month 8 you learned how to guide your teams through the sometimes rough waters of dealing with internal suppliers. By this time your teams members should have identified their suppliers and met with at least one supplier to establish joint goals and determine what each group must do to achieve those goals.

It's now time for your teams to work on the flip side of the customer-supplier relationship—becoming better suppliers to their customers. Your teams might be unaware of problems they are causing their internal customers. Help your teams evaluate their role as supplier by following the two-step process introduced in New Team Month 8 (pages 174-175). First ask the team to identify up to four internal groups to whom they provide information, services, or products.

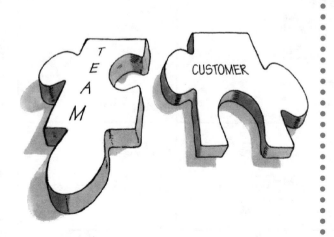

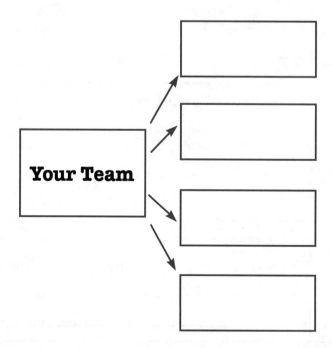

Next, ask your teams to meet with one internal customer, establish a joint goal, and identify what each group must do to achieve the goal. The following sample agreement form was developed by a manufacturing team (the supplier) and a sales group (the customer).

Sample Agreement Form

Joint Goal	Team Needs	Internal Customer Needs	Agreements
Deliver products to the end-user customer on time.	• *Real, not exaggerated, delivery dates.* • *Honest labeling of rush jobs.*	• *Consistent track record of on-time delivery.* • *Immediate communication if there's a chance of a delay.*	• *Manufacturing team member (Bob) will ride with Ted next week to talk directly to customers.* • *Sales and manufacturing members will exchange phone numbers to improve communication.* • *Production star point will wear a beeper.* • *Manufacturing and sales will meet at end of quarter to review on-time delivery performance and the sales pipeline.*

Additional Issues

Help your teams anticipate their internal customers' needs and concerns. Coach the team members through these questions:

- What do internal customers do with our products or services?

- What are their jobs?

- What do we do that helps them reach their goals?

- What do we do that might cause problems for them?

Remember: Knowing how a customer uses your teams' products or services can help your teams understand the customers' needs and identify possible improvements.

Week 4
Getting out of meetings

We know what you're thinking . . . and no, we're not suggesting this just to give you a way out of attending boring, purposeless meetings. No one should have to waste their time in unproductive meetings, especially not your team members.

Actually, there are several legitimate reasons for having team members attend meetings in your place:

- Topics that have become routine for you might be educational for them.

- They are closer to the problems and actual functioning of the core process than you are.

- It would give them visibility with other managers and leaders and with customers and suppliers.

- It would free you to do things that would add more value to your job and the teams' operations.

Selecting the Right Meeting

Complete the following form to identify those meetings you could transfer to team members.

1. List the meetings you typically attend (column 1).

2. Use the following scale to rate the meeting on three factors—educational value (column 2), the value of a detailed understanding of the team's work (column 3), and exposure value (column 4):
   1 = Low   2 = Moderate   3 = High

3. Add up the values (columns 2, 3, and 4) you've assigned to the meeting. Write the total in column 5.

4. Consider sending a team member to the meeting with the highest value, as indicated in column 5.

1 Regular Meetings	2 Educational Value	3 Process Understanding	4 Exposure/ Visibility Value	5 Total

Transfering Responsibility for the Meeting

Do the following to transfer this meeting to a team member:

1. Clear the proposal with the meeting leader.

   - Explain why this will benefit the meeting process.

   - Establish a mechanism for you to get needed information.

   - Agree to attend when needed.

2. Identify a team member who could benefit and contribute.

   - Ask for volunteers.

   - Or identify someone who would naturally contribute or benefit the most (one of the star point roles, for instance).

3. Provide coaching.

   - Review the meeting's purpose and the last three agendas or sets of minutes.

   - Provide background on the other attendees.

   - Discuss the team member's role in the meeting.

     —Communicate information *from* the team.

     —Communicate information *to* the team.

     —Identify problems.

     —Solve problems.

     —Support the team's needs and interests.

   - Openly discuss problems.

   - Identify any work that must be done before and after the meeting.

   - Agree on the support you'll provide.

     —Attend with the team member for _____ meetings.

     —Debrief after the first _____ meetings.

     —Attend the meeting when needed.

4. Set a follow-up date to evaluate how the arrangement is working.

5. Identify something you will do instead of attending the meeting:

Month 9

Notes. . .

When to Call for Help

- Some team leaders have a hard time objectively evaluating their teams' meeting dynamics. If you're unsure about your ability to remain objective, you might want to ask for help from an outside facilitator or trainer.

- If you anticipate a particularly difficult meeting between your team and its internal customer, you might want to ask for an external "referee."

If You Do Nothing Else . . .

1. Analyze one team's meeting process and provide feedback.

2. Find at least two ways to reinforce training the team has already completed.

3. Coach your team through an analysis of at least one customer's needs.

Month at a Glance

MONDAY	TUESDAY	WEDNESDAY	THURSDAY	FRIDAY	SATURDAY/ SUNDAY
Analyze team meeting process —1 hour		Coach team member to analyze meetings —2 hours		Conduct team skills training for new hires —4 hours	
	Identify ways to reinforce training —1 hour				
Check progress with manager —1 hour			Lead team through customer analysis —1 hour		
Identify what meetings to transfer —1 hour		Coach team member to attend meeting —1 hour	Coach team member on action items after meeting —1 hour		

Time Budget

	Goal	Actual
Team coaching	55%	
Project work	15%	
Administrative	15%	
Personal development	15%	

Key Lessons

_____

_____

_____

_____

_____

_____

Next Steps

_____

_____

_____

_____

_____

_____

New Team Month 10

Notes. . .

Month 10

What to Expect

Your teams now are more stable. They are becoming increasingly self-directed. This means you probably have more time to focus on other issues and concerns. One of those issues is your own development. Because your role is changing dramatically, you will want to start considering development activities that will enhance your performance as a leader of teams. This month you can start doing that.

Larry in Limbo

Recently, Larry discovered that he wasn't as busy as he used to be. Ten months ago he was overwhelmed by all the issues that came with the move to teams. Then there was arranging all that training for team members and following up with coaching and support. But lately Larry has found that he actually has some free time. He wasn't even aware of the extra time on his hands until this week when his manager found him reading a newspaper in his office at 10 a.m. Larry figured he better get busy doing something (but what?) before management decided he was expendable. The teams were handling most of their new administrative responsibilities well, so they didn't need his constant attention and coaching. Maybe, Larry thought, there's something I should be doing to increase my knowledge and skills, and my value to the organization.

Possible Concerns

Recently one of our team members retired. Although the rest of the team was involved in selecting a new member, something is not right. Their meetings aren't as productive as they used to be and there's more conflict than ever before.

After nine months of working together, the original team members were developing a groove. They understood each other's styles and preferences, and they had figured out how to work with each other. A new member can upset those dynamics.

This reaction has long been recognized in management teams. That's why many organizations use a process called an "inclusion meeting" when a new manager joins a group. The purpose of the meeting is to accelerate everyone's comfort and acceptance of the new member. You might borrow this technique for your own team:

1. Ask an outside facilitator to interview team members to find out what they'd like to know about the new member.

2. If your team uses some form of style assessment, ask the new member to complete the assessment.

3. The outside facilitator begins the meeting by asking the current members to introduce themselves, explaining their roles in the team, style, etc.

4. The new member is given some time to talk about other experiences, style, feelings about joining the team, etc. The new member then asks questions about the team's history or practices. The team can use this time to review its operating guidelines and update them, if appropriate.

5. The facilitator asks the new member the questions that were collected from the team, ensuring that everyone's issues and concerns are addressed.

It also may be appropriate to review the team's charter and training schedule. All of this should help the new member become assimilated and get your team back on track.

Your Focus This Month

Most of this month is focused on your own development. You will have opportunities to:

- Meet with your manager.

- Prepare yourself for the transition to a more advanced role.

- Help teams learn from and rectify mistakes.

- Learn from other leaders.

Week 1
Checkpoint #5: What's your next move?

All along you should have been meeting regularly with your manager to review your progress as well as your teams'. But now that the teams have passed their nine-month mark, you and your manager need to hold a career review discussion.

What's Your Next Move?

To prepare for that discussion, think about what you want to do with your extra time. Consider what you enjoy doing, what you're good at doing, and what the organization needs. Most leaders find that they have a few fundamental choices:

1. **Lead more teams.**

   Example: Anne went from leading two new customer service teams (with a total of 18 people) to three mature teams (27 people) and one new team (8 people).

2. **Initiate cross-team projects.**

   Example: Roger continued to facilitate two mature teams but spent the rest of his time (50 percent) with the research and development department on new product development.

3. **Become a full-time trainer or team facilitator.**

   Example: Carlos moved out of manufacturing and joined a small group of team trainers in human resources. He now spends all his time coaching and training teams.

4. **Move into a technical contributor role.**

   Example: Sue believed she wasn't suited for leading teams, so she went back to the engineering group as a full-time industrial engineer.

Check with your manager to find out if the options you considered in the Preteam Phase still make sense and to get feedback on your manager's perception of where you can make the greatest contribution.

Of course, you also want to consider your personal preferences before making a decision. Your views about these options may have changed as you've gained more experience with teams.

Considering Options

Completing the form on page 199 will help you weigh your training and career options. If you don't know enough about an option to make an informed choice, interview or shadow someone doing the job.

After you narrow your options, plan specific developmental activities so that you're ready to make the transition when your team no longer needs your day-to-day leadership. ➤

Career Options	Option open to me? Yes? No?	Pros: Things I like about doing this/ My strengths in this area	Cons: Things I don't like about doing this/ My weaknesses in this area
1. Lead more teams.			
2. Initiate cross-team projects.			
3. Become a full-time trainer or team facilitator.			
4. Move into a technical contributor role. List top two jobs:			

Date for meeting with your manager: _____

Week 2
Life after coaching: Advancing your role

By now you (with your manager's help) should have narrowed your career options. The next step is to plan specific developmental activities to help you advance your role.

The four options introduced last week are included on this and the next page. Select the one you will focus on, review the sample development activities, add others you and your manager consider appropriate, and set a completion date for the development activity.

Option	Development Activities	Completion Date
1. Lead more teams. Major challenges: Time management and focus.	☐ Attend a time management class. ☐ Interview/Shadow a leader who handles several teams. Collect tips and techniques. ☐ Sharpen delegation skills. ☐ Other ideas:	
2. Initiate cross-team projects. Major challenges: Requires a new set of skills (sales, project tracking, initiative, etc.).	☐ Attend a project management class. ☐ Learn a project management software package. ☐ Start a file of potential project ideas. ☐ Ask to participate on a high-level project team with a skilled project leader. ☐ Other ideas:	

Option	Development Activities	Completion Date
3. Full-time trainer or team facilitator Major challenges: Need for excellent platform and process observation skills.	☐ Seek training certification from your organization's team training vendor. ☐ Ask to deliver training jointly with an outstanding trainer. ☐ Read about group and team dynamics. ☐ Sign up for an organizational development course at the local college. ☐ Other ideas:	
4. Become a technical contributor Major challenges: Need to become reacquainted with advancements in the functional area you've chosen.	☐ Ask to be assigned to a part-time project in your chosen area. ☐ Ask an incumbent in the area for advice on how to bring yourself up to date. ☐ Ask to attend departmental meetings in your chosen area. ☐ Subscribe to a pertinent technical journal. ☐ Other ideas:	

Week 3
Oops!—When a team makes a major mistake

Although major mistakes could happen anytime, they are very common in the teams' first year—when their eagerness may outstrip their experience. Major mistakes could include anything from missing a key customer requirement to implementing a process improvement that backfires. A lot will depend on your organization's tolerance for mistakes.

Use the following five-step flowchart to analyze the mistake and help your team benefit from the experience.

Step 1

Does the team realize they made a mistake?

Yes

Evaluate the effect of the mistake on the team:

Devastated ◄────► *Unconcerned*

Help the team reach a state of constructive concern.

No

Help the team get feedback about the mistake as soon as possible. If possible, arrange for the team to hear about the problem from the group it affected the most.

Step 2

Has the team rectified the mistake to the best of their ability?

Yes

Reinforce the team for taking action. Help them assess whether there is anything else the organization should do. There could be avenues for recovery or restitution that are beyond the team's control.

No

Involve the team as much as possible in fixing the mistake. Not only will it help them learn, but it will help them put the mistake behind them.

Step 3

Has the team made this or a similar mistake before?

Yes

This is evidence of a serious problem (lack of learning, a previous solution that isn't working, or a performance problem on the team). The team may not be capable of correcting this problem on their own. This requires your close intervention.

No

Don't over react. If you punish them for a first-time occurrence, they may stop taking initiative or start covering up their mistakes.

Step 4

Has the team accurately pinpointed the cause of the mistake?

Yes

Reinforce the team for its initiative.

No

Coach the team through the use of cause analysis tools (Pareto charts, fish bone diagrams, etc.). Do not do the work for them.

Step 5

Has the team identified a reliable system for preventing this (or a related) mistake from happening again?

Yes

Help the team implement any necessary changes in systems or training.

No

Help the team brainstorm and test alternatives. Don't create new policies and procedures if you don't have to.

General Guidelines to Help Teams Learn from Their Experiences

- Stop protecting the team from direct feedback. Gradually remove barriers; allow the teams to feel the consequences of their actions—both good and bad—more directly.

- Devote time at each team meeting to lessons learned (or create a "lessons learned" board). Plan for specific things you will do differently as a result of lessons learned each week.

- When analyzing mistakes focus on the systems and processes, not the people.

- Celebrate initiative; discourage covering up.

- Periodically review lessons learned.

- Identify conditions that lead to making mistakes. Periodically evaluate whether any of these conditions are present on the team.

Week 4
Learning from other leaders

Many leaders believe that the only way to learn about teams is through trial and error. Although they might meet regularly with other leaders, those meetings usually focus on business results or technical problems. The leaders rarely discuss team problems and potential solutions.

Why Reinvent the Wheel?

The irony is that 80 percent of the team problems that arise have been faced and solved by other leaders. Yet many leaders are trying to come up with their own solutions to problems—they are continually reinventing the wheel!

Much of this unnecessary work could be avoided if leaders held regular forums for sharing and discussing common issues and problems. These forums could be support groups (a type of "Autocrats Anonymous," for instance), monthly brown-bag lunches, or quarterly informal gatherings (a sort of "Leaders Night Out"). If such a group does not exist within your organization, take the initiative now to set one up. You can model your forum on this sample charter:

Autocrats Anonymous

Purpose: To help leaders of teams kick the autocratic habit by creating a forum to share and discuss team leadership problems.

Membership: All first-line leaders of teams.

Ground rules: We agree to create a safe environment for discussing problems by:

- Openly sharing our own experiences.
- Maintaining confidentiality.
- Respecting each other's perspectives.
- Focusing on the problem, not the person.
- Avoiding blaming others.

Meetings: Second and fourth Friday of every month from noon to 1:30.

A typical agenda for this type of leader forum is illustrated below:

Sample Agenda

12:00	*Follow up on problems/solutions discussed at last meeting: Are they working?*
12:20	*Round-robin listing of new problems/ concerns/issues.*
12:30	*Select top two to discuss.*
12:35	*Form two subgroups to discuss and identify three alternative solutions.*
1:10	*Subgroup reports.*
1:25	*Other issues.*

Your Approach

Would such a forum be useful/possible in your organization?

☐ Yes

If you answered Yes:

1. Who do you need to contact to get it started?

2. How often would you recommend meeting?

3. Who would be involved (excluded from) the meetings?

4. When will you start?

☐ No

If you answered No:

Other alternatives for learning from each other include (select at least one):

☐ A buddy system.

☐ Switching teams for a week.

☐ An e-mail box for anonymous "Leaders' Lessons Learned."

Notes. . .

Month 10

When to Call for Help

- If you have a mentor in the organization— someone whose advice and perspective you respect—you may want to consult him or her about your career options and development before you meet with your manager.

- If you're having trouble drumming up support for a leaders' network, you might need to ask for help from the sponsor for the change. It may be easier to sell the idea of a few trial meetings to let people try the idea on for size.

If You Do Nothing Else . . .

1. Assess your own career preferences and then check these with the organization.

2. Begin active development for the next phase of your leadership career.

3. Check to make sure you are helping your teams learn from their experiences.

Month at a Glance

MONDAY	TUESDAY	WEDNESDAY	THURSDAY	FRIDAY	SATURDAY/ SUNDAY
	Assess career options, plan development —2 hours			Check results against baseline —1 hour	
		Meet with manager —3 hours		Update file of possible project ideas —1 hour	
Help team to analyze—and learn from—a mistake —2 hours				Mini Team Celebration —15 minutes	
			Plan leader network —1 hour		

Time Budget

	Goal	Actual
Team coaching	50%	
Project work	20%	
Administrative	15%	
Personal development	15%	

Key Lessons

_____

_____

_____

_____

_____

Next Steps

_____

_____

_____

_____

_____

207

New Team Month 11

Notes. . .

What to Expect

It should be getting relatively easy to work with your teams. They handle many responsibilities on their own, and yet they still seem to appreciate your coaching and feedback around their team and interpersonal development. Usually the only dangers at this point are stagnation and complacency.

Possible Concerns

I just found out I'm picking up responsibility for another team this month. How can I give both teams the attention they need?

You need a plan. Effective team leaders often find that they have to maintain a list of issues and development steps for each team. No two teams are at the same stage of development or have the same needs. However, if you start each week with a particular development goal for each team, you'll find that you can help more than one team at a time advance effectively.

Consider creating a development schedule such as the sample below. Because your new team probably will require more attention, be sure to discuss this fact openly with your established teams. Work out a plan so that you are available when they really need help.

Sample Weekly Team Development Plan

	Development Goals	Actions
Established Teams		
–K25	*Better understanding of customer requirements.*	*Coach team to start responding directly to customer complaint letters.*
–IB12	*More equal involvement of all team members.*	*Coach Lee on how to get Anne and Pat to participate more in team meetings.*
New Team		
–SR78	*Technical flexibility.*	*• Help the team find time for cross-training.* *• Follow up with Jerry on the cross-training plan.*
	Following agendas in team meetings.	*• Coach Eduardo in advance of meeting.* *• Sit in on meeting.* *• Provide feedback after meeting.*

Your Focus This Month

This month you should set aside time to:

- Ask for feedback from your teams.

- Help your teams make better decisions.

- Provide coaching that is tailored to each person.

- Encourage team initiative.

Week 1
Asking for feedback from the teams

Most leaders go through their entire careers suffering from "blind spots": Problems that are obvious to others but to which the leaders themselves are oblivious. You know this is true because you and your fellow leaders have definite opinions about the flaws and foibles of your managers. So, too, do your team members have important perspectives and observations about your behavior.

If you can tap into these perspectives and improve your behavior, it will be an invaluable boost to your career and to the effectiveness of the teams within your area.

How to Get Feedback

There are three basic approaches for gathering team member feedback.

1. **Anonymous survey**

    Team members complete an anonymous survey or scorecard rating your leadership behavior. A neutral party collects and scores the surveys. You receive the combined results.

Pro: The feedback you get will probably be honest.

Con: Unless the survey was prepared by a professional, the results may be difficult to interpret or understand.

2. **Ombudsman**

Team members pick a trusted third party to collect the feedback. This person interviews all team members and funnels the feedback to you without attributing it to any particular person.

Pro: You can follow up and ask questions to be sure you understand.

Con: • Team members might not be completely honest with a third person.

• The "trusted third party" might put his or her own twist on the feedback.

3. Face-to-face with team members

You openly solicit feedback in a meeting with team members.

Pro: This approach models above-board, adult interactions.

Con: You might not get honest negative feedback.

Selecting a Feedback Method

Follow these steps to choose one of the three feedback methods.

1. Add your own pros and cons for each method.

2. Eliminate any method you are uncomfortable with.

3. Review the remaining options with the team:

   a. Discuss how the feedback will benefit you and the team.

   b. Make a commitment to act on the feedback.

   c. Encourage the team members to tell you what they see as each method's pros and cons.

   d. Select an option.

4. Schedule the feedback.

5. Schedule a follow-up meeting with the team to review the feedback and what you are doing about it.

Week 2
Helping your teams make better decisions

One of the main reasons organizations resist empowering teams fully is that they're afraid the teams will make bad decisions. It's your job to see that this excuse does not get in the way of your teams' empowerment. You can do that by coaching your teams to make effective decisions.

Analyze the major decisions your teams have made during the last ten months. Record your thoughts on the form on the next page. You also can use this form as the basis for a team meeting on decision making—involving the team in analyzing its own decision-making process. Use the following example as a guide.

In this example, it's clear that the team often failed to consult with other groups. Yet, the information shows that when the team did involve others, the results were positive. Look for similar patterns with your teams.

Sample Team Decision Grid

Team decisions	Results of decision	Was decision good or bad, and why?
Technical *Shut down press for four hours on January 12.*	*$110,000 in production lost, but nothing was found to be wrong.*	*Bad decision: Maintenance wasn't consulted first.*
Customer/Supplier *Worked overtime to ship 12 extra pallets to Acme.*	*Acme didn't need them; sent them back.*	*Bad decision: Made assumption, didn't check with sales.*
Team Management *Lobbied for additional training on conflict resolution.*	*Got training; became model for other teams.*	*Good decision: It worked because human resources was involved from the start.*

Your Team Decision Grid

Team decisions	Results of decision	Was decision good or bad, and why?
Technical		
Customer/Supplier		
Team Management		

Week 3
Providing tailor-made coaching

Leaders often have difficulty coaching the very best performers and the weakest performers. Leaders tend to neglect top performers because they assume these people can fend for themselves. On the other hand, leaders typically avoid weak performers because . . . well, it's unfortunate, but true, interactions with them usually are not very rewarding. Nevertheless, both of these groups need your help.

Weak Performer

Answer the questions on this page to describe a team member who is performing below par. Use the example provided in italics to help you consider the possibilities in your teams.

1. Identify a team member whose performance needs to be improved.

   Bob

   In your teams:

2. The difficulty in coaching poor performers is that you have so much to do but so little time to do it all. To help you get started, identify just one behavior that needs to be improved.

   Stop putting down other people's ideas in meetings.

   In your teams:

3. Prepare to have a coaching discussion with this person. How will you describe the problem?

   People look up to you, and when you put down their ideas, it causes them to clam up.

   In your teams:

4. How will you ask about possible causes of the problem?

Why do you do it?

In your teams:

5. What possible solutions come to mind?

   I could provide a reminder before each meeting.

   In your teams:

6. When do you want to follow up to see how the solutions are working?

   Right after next Tuesday's meeting.

   In your teams:

Strong Performer

Top performers need encouragement to stretch beyond their current accomplishments. Respond to the following statements to describe a team member who is performing above par. Use the example provided in italics to identify a situation in your teams.

1. Identify a team member whose performance has been above average.

   Karen

   In your teams:

2. Pinpoint a particular strength or talent and how you will reinforce that strength:

   Is a whiz at quantitative analysis and first on team to master statistical process control. Nominating for an internship in accounting.

   In your teams:

3. Pick an opportunity for them to stretch or develop the skill in a way that benefits them and the team.

   Lead the team through an analysis of team expenses for the last three years to identify chronic variances.

In your teams:

4. Plan what support you will need to provide.

   Help gather figures from accounting; review last year's analysis.

   In your teams:

5. Set a date for approaching the person about the opportunity.

   Friday after the team meeting.

   In your teams:

Use the form provided to identify your strong and weak performers and to schedule coaching sessions.

	Date for Initial Coaching	Follow-up Date
Strong Performer		
Weak Performer		

Week 4
Encouraging team initiative

The Self-propelled Team

Now's a good time to reinforce your teams' skills in generating their own ideas and improvements. This not only will make your job much easier, but it also will greatly enhance the teams' overall performance. It's the difference between crossing the lake in rowboat or in a speedboat with a 300–horsepower motor. You need a self-propelled team!

Undermining Initiative: A Survey

Many factors affect team initiative. One of the most significant is the leader's behavior. Many team leaders inadvertently squelch the natural initiative that exists in new teams. They don't mean to do it, they just don't know any better. Do you encourage team initiative, or are you a wet blanket at the party?

Answer the following questions. You also might want to distribute copies of these questions to your team members and ask them to respond to them. Compare their responses with yours to see how you stack up in the eyes of the people you should be encouraging. Check all that apply.

Do you ever:

☐ Veto an idea because it didn't work in the past?

☐ Judge an idea before the person who originated the idea is finished explaining it?

☐ Present team members' ideas to other people without giving them credit?

☐ Fail to give team members full attention when they're explaining ideas?

☐ Promise to get back to a team member about an idea and then forget to do so?

☐ Discourage good, workable ideas because you know they'll be difficult to implement?

If you or your teams have checked two or more items, you need to fix your own behavior before working with the teams on their initiative.

Promoting Initiative: A List of Ideas

Even if you're not actively smothering initiative, you may not be aggressively promoting it either. If that's the case, review this list of ideas for encouraging team initiative. Check those you don't already do, and try to implement three of them this week.

☐ Devote time at each meeting to discuss ideas and improvement opportunities.

☐ Keep the team informed of organizational goals and changes. (Remember: It's hard to act when you're in the dark.)

☐ Provide resources (time, materials, access to others) that team members need to develop or implement ideas.

☐ Help teams brainstorm alternatives for established procedures, processes, and jobs on your team.

☐ Encourage and celebrate small improvements.

☐ Use "what if" questions to get the team thinking about nontraditional approaches.

Notes. . .

Month 11

When to Call for Help

- If you're having trouble objectively analyzing your teams' decision-making patterns and processes—that is, you can't see any room for improvement—you may want to ask for outside help. Sometimes if you and another team leader switch teams, it's easier to spot opportunities for improvement.

- If you're having difficulty collecting feedback from your teams, check with your human resources department—it may have some excellent tools or suggestions.

If You Do Nothing Else . . .

1. Explain to the team why it's important for you to receive feedback and agree on a process for collecting the feedback that everyone feels comfortable with.

2. Help your teams become more independent and productive by analyzing and developing their abilities to make decisions and take initiative.

3. Raise overall team performance through one-on-one coaching sessions with the top and bottom performers.

Month at a Glance

MONDAY	TUESDAY	WEDNESDAY	THURSDAY	FRIDAY	SATURDAY/ SUNDAY
Contract with team for feedback —1 hour		Add ideas to potential project file —1 hour		Get feedback from the team —2 hours	
	Analyze team decisions —2 hours	Give team feedback on decisions —1 hour			
Identify strong/weak performers —2 hours		Coach weak performer —1 hour		Coach top performer —1 hour	
	Analyze team initiative —1 hour		First leader network meeting —1 hour	Review progress with manager —1 hour	

Time Budget

	Goal	Actual
Team coaching	50%	
Project work	20%	
Administrative	10%	
Personal development	20%	

Key Lessons

_____
_____
_____
_____
_____
_____
_____

Next Steps

_____
_____
_____
_____
_____
_____
_____

New Team Month 12

What to Expect

Now that your teams are proceeding on a steady course, you can enjoy the sense of accomplishment that comes from taking a loose collection of individuals and transforming them into a high-performance team.

Possible Concerns

Can I relax now that my teams have made it? Is there any chance that they'll slip back into a more primitive stage of development?

Sorry. You can't put your feet up yet. We've seen quite a few teams lose ground when:

- One or more members develop a serious personal problem.

- Several members leave the team over a short period of time.

- Management commitment for teams fades.

- Team members have been overworked or become burned out.

- Members become overconfident and stop working on team development.

For these reasons it's a good idea to measure your teams' development at regular intervals, typically every three to six months. Measuring their development will help keep you aware of the factors that are likely to affect your teams' progress.

Your Focus This Month

As your teams wind up this phase, you will want to focus your energies on:

- Conducting a team health check.

- Developing a broader business perspective.

- Renewing commitment to the team process.

- Celebrating progress.

Week 1
Taking the teams' temperature—Part 2

It's been nearly nine months since your last formal team check-up, so now's a good time to have your teams check their progress. Because your teams will be taking a more active role in monitoring their development and checking their progress, you should be preparing them for that responsibility now. You can do that by coaching the teams on how to handle the monitoring process on their own. Follow these steps:

1. Help the teams apply continuous improvement principles. Ask someone in each team to lead the team through an analysis of what worked and what didn't work in the last health check. Help the team plan an improved process.

2. Agree on what to evaluate. Remind the teams that to get an accurate reading on progress, they must include the same factors used in the first check-up (see pages 112-113):

   • Purpose

   • Process

   • Communication

   • Commitment

   • Involvement

   • Trust

But they might want to add others, such as:

   • **Learning,** or the extent to which the team members are continuing to develop and benefit from their mistakes.

   • **Self-directedness,** that is, the level of responsibility the team has assumed for its own management, technical processes, and business results.

3. Coach the teams through planning and scheduling the evaluation process.

4. Offer to give the teams feedback on their handling of the evaluation process.

5. Help the teams schedule a regular review process for at least the next year.

Debriefing Your Behavior

While coaching the teams on conducting their own check-ups, did you:

☐ Support the teams without removing their responsibility for taking action?

☐ Account for less than 10 percent air time in all the meetings?

☐ Let the teams to do it their way as long as it would work, even if their approach wasn't your first choice.

Week 2
Developing a broader business perspective

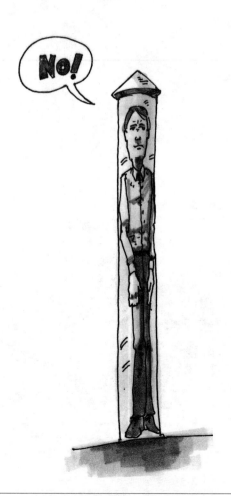

Your Shifting Focus

Over time most leaders find that their roles shift from one that focuses on internal team issues to one that concentrates on broader business issues.

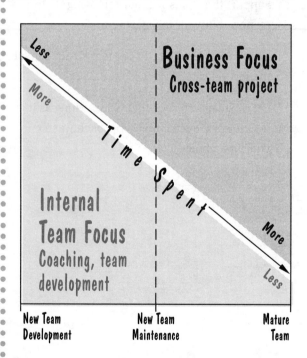

Where Are You?

It's not too soon to prepare yourself for this shift. Most leaders are handicapped by coming up through the ranks in one particular functional silo. This experience greatly limits their perspective on problems and issues the organization is facing.

Thinking Like a Manager

You will increase your value to the organization immeasurably if you can begin to think like a general manager. Some of the things general managers do that might help you include:

- Subscribing to industry publications.

- Attending industry conferences.

- Networking.

  —Contacting a variety of people inside and outside the organization to sample viewpoints; probing and listening for trends and new ideas.

  —Collecting feedback from trusted colleagues on ideas; putting forth trial concepts.

  —Talking directly to customers about their needs and requirements.

- Staying on top of regulatory influences and government policy changes. (There are publications that monitor these trends for most industries and functions.)

- Understanding competitive forces, including strengths and weaknesses of rival organizations (often by talking to your own sales and marketing people).

Add your own ideas

Select two of the above strategies and make them part of your daily job. To ensure that your strategies are paying off, pick a day three months from now, (note it on your calendar) and evaluate how well these approaches are working for you. At that time you can change your approach or add new strategies.

Week 3
Renewing the teams

You've been working in teams for almost a year now. It's easy to lose sight of why you started this journey in the first place. Now is a good time to reexamine the original purpose for teams and recommit to the team process.

This can take place at the organizational level or, if your organization doesn't have anything planned, right at your own team level.

Consider the following possible renewal activities. Use these to plan your own renewal event on the facing page.

Menu of Possible Renewal Activities

- Invite a customer to talk about the positive impact your teams have had on the customer's business.

- Ask the site manager or sponsor of the change to discuss the direction for the facility and how teams fit into the future of the business.

- Ask team members to create two large collages: one depicting the group before teams and one representing the group after teams.

- Ask team members to put together a skit showing the group's progress.

- Plan to review and update the teams' charters (with each team member leading the discussion of one section).

- Ask all team members to sign a poster-size copy of their team's charter.

- Plan a team open house so that other employees and family members can tour your area and learn about the teams' progress.

- Evaluate the teams' development and plan additional training.

Use the following example as a guide to assemble your own renewal plan.

7:00 a.m.	*Post "before" and "after" collages of the team*
7:15 a.m.	*Break out the donuts and host an open house consisting of:*
	• *Tours*
	• *Posters*
	• *Suggestion box*
2:00 p.m.	*Ron from Acme Service comes in*
2:20 p.m.	*Site manager*
2:40 p.m.	*We review and revise our charter*
3:15 p.m.	*New charter signing ceremony*

Your renewal plan

Consider what else you will need to do to plan an effective team renewal activity and develop your own preparation checklist.

Things To Do

☐ Get my manager's approval.

☐ Pick a date:_____

☐ Involve the team.

☐ Communicate what we are doing to the rest of the organization.

☐ Arrange coverage for team members who will be participating in the renewal activity.

My Preparation Checklist

☐

☐

☐

☐

☐

Week 4
Celebrating progress

The last time you and your teams held a celebration, it was to mark the teams' accomplishments. Now that you are about to change your role and give the teams more responsibility for self-management, you should help the teams celebrate progress they've made in their development. Complete the following assessment to plan a meaningful celebration of team progress.

Assessing the Last Celebration

Look back at the last celebration. Help the team analyze what worked and what didn't work. Assess that celebration to determine what you can do to give this celebration meaning and what you want to avoid doing. Write everyone's thoughts on a chart like the one below.

What Worked	What Didn't Work
Everyone agreed that the outside speakers had the most impact.	*Held celebration on Friday–our busiest day—so everyone felt pressured to get back to work.*

Cataloging Team Achievements

Read the following examples of team accomplishments. Some of them might apply to your teams' situation. Use them to help your teams identify their own developmental accomplishments.

Examples of Team Development	Your Teams' Accomplishments
• *Team completed cross-training matrix.* • *Team took responsibility for running all its own meetings. Attendance at meetings now 100 percent.* • *Team had 20 percent more improvement suggestions over last six months.* • *Team openly discussing tough issues in team meetings (theft example).*	

How to Celebrate

Some ways to celebrate developmental accomplishments include:

- A mock graduation ceremony.

- A team dinner, with the highest-ranking site manager offering a toast to the team.

- A humorous retrospective look at the team ("then" and "now").

- A round-robin discussion in which all team members comment on what they like about working in the team now.

Consider these, along with the recognition ideas on page 180. Using this form, involve team members in planning the celebration.

What to Celebrate	How to Celebrate	When to Celebrate

Notes. . .

Month 12

When to Call for Help

If you're already doing many of the things outlined on pages 224 and 225 to develop a broader business perspective and need some fresh ideas, schedule several short meetings with managers you respect. Ask them how they stay on top of the business. Most managers will be flattered that you asked for their advice, and they'll be happy to help.

If You Do Nothing Else . . .

1. Have the teams check their own progress.

2. Help team members renew their commitment to the team concept.

3. Coach team members in arranging a celebration of their accomplishments.

Month at a Glance

MONDAY	TUESDAY	WEDNESDAY	THURSDAY	FRIDAY	SATURDAY/ SUNDAY
Coach members for team check-up —1 hour		Plan renewal event —1 hour		Observe team as part of check-up —2 hours	
	Plan how to develop broader business perspective —1 hour		Meet with colleagues; discuss business trends —1 hour	Add to project idea file —1 hour	
Coach teams through preparation for renewal event —1 hour				Team renewal event —4 hours	
			Team Celebration —1 hour		

Time Budget

	Goal	Actual
Team coaching	45%	
Project work	25%	
Administrative	10%	
Personal development	20%	

Key Lessons

_____
_____
_____
_____
_____
_____

Next Steps

_____
_____
_____
_____
_____
_____
_____

Notes...

Mature Team Phase

For some 12 months you've been guiding your teams through the unfamiliar waters of high-performance teams. They now have the skills not only to survive, but to flourish. It's time for you to go on to new challenges. Use the activities outlined over the next few months to continue developing your own role.

Month 1

- Changing your role (again)
- Checking your changing role
- Branching out (developing lateral focus)
- Helping your teams from a distance

Month 2

- Doing an environment scan
- Reassessing your own training needs
- Developing external partnerships
- Getting organizational approval

Month 3

- Identifying cross-team projects
- Assessing your initiative
- Checkpoint #6: Touching base with your manager
- Turning over final responsibilities to the teams

Month 4

- Assessing your project management skills
- Cost-benefit analysis
- Developing proposals for new business
- Taking stock of your own progress

Mature Team Month 1

Notes. . .

Month 1

What to Expect

Your teams should be approaching the fourth stage in team development, Full Speed Ahead. They've probably taken on most of the planned responsibilities, and their performance should have stabilized.

4. Full Speed Ahead

1. Getting Started

2. Going in Circles

3. Getting on Course

You should find that you don't have to spend as much time coaching and guiding them on day-to-day tasks. This means you should have time to spend on more proactive, strategic tasks.

Possible Concerns

I was very comfortable in my role. I was getting good at coaching the team. Now you're telling me more changes are on the way. What if I don't like, or can't master, this more advanced role?

Your feelings are completely natural. Almost everyone has the same concern. In fact, you probably felt a lot like this 12 months ago when you were faced with making the transition from your traditional role to a leader of teams.

Think about the survival techniques you used to make it through that transition: getting training, planning how to spend your time differently, talking with others making the same transition, etc. Many of the same techniques will be just as helpful now.

Give the new role a chance. If you find that you're not suited to the project focus of the new role, you should have plenty of other opportunities to do what you excel at. You could help start new teams, take full-time responsibility for training teams, or even carve a role as a facilitator-at-large.

I'm ready for this transition, but my teams aren't. Actually, I think they're ready; they just don't realize it. They don't seem to want to give up having me around all the time.

First, examine your own behavior. Are you doing anything that fosters dependence on you: Doing their thinking for them? Fixing things for them? Communicating their concerns to others?

Next, objectively assess whether you might be trying to push them out of the nest too early. Some teams don't mature as quickly as others. With your teams, list the things they need to do on their own before you can move into your new role. Then plan exactly what help they need to reach that point.

If a team is ready but just doesn't want to let go, discuss the situation openly with them. For instance, remind the team that, while you were on vacation, they handled everything capably. Make specific commitments to them about your availability. Offer to reassess how the transition is working after two weeks.

Your Focus This Month

Most of this month you will be focusing on activities that affect your role. You will be concentrating on:

- Changing your role (again).

- Getting input from your manager, the teams, and others on your changing role.

- Becoming more aware of lateral relationships within the organization.

- How you can help your teams from a distance.

Week 1
Changing your role (again)

As teams mature, many leaders find that their own roles change. During the New Team Phase, leaders focus primarily on the teams' development. But during this Mature Team Phase efforts are often concentrated on issues outside the teams. ➤

New Team Phase	Mature Team Phase
Focus is on the teams.	Focus is on projects and improvements.
Concern about what's going on inside the teams.	Concern about what's going on in the organization or business.
Planning is day-to-day or week-to-week.	Planning involves projects over many months.

This radical change in focus translates into a significant difference in how leaders spend their time. Consider how one leader's typical days changed when her teams matured:

One day in the life of a new team leader	
7:00 a.m.	*Sit in on team meeting: facilitate closure, take two action items*
8:00	*Walk around teams' areas: help get replacement worker*
9:30	*Attend production meeting*
10:30	*Help team fix major equipment problem*
12:00 p.m.	*Take supplier to lunch*
1:00	*Help team member resolve conflict with another area*
1:30	*Coach team safety coordinator for plantwide presentation*
2:15	*Provide input to area budget*
2:45	*Follow up on equipment problem*
3:00	*Provide corrective coaching on a housekeeping problem*
3:30	*Facilitate shift-to-shift communication*
4:00	*Complete paperwork*

One day in the life of a mature team leader	
7:00 a.m.	*Sit in on team meeting: reinforce members, talk about your project*
8:00	*Head task force meeting on new packaging material*
9:30	*Interview three new packaging vendors*
11:00	*Discuss packaging problems with corporate purchasing department*
12:00 p.m.	*Lunch with plant purchasing specialist to plot strategy*
1:00	*Revise new packaging changeover schedule*
1:30	*Help team member with a new supplier problem*
2:00	*Attend expansion task force meeting*
3:00	*Update team on expansion plans*
3:20	*Coach team members before interviewing new team member candidates*
4:00	*Think about better ways to serve the customer*

Become More Project Focused

To prepare for this role change, answer the following questions:

What three improvements would you like to make at your site?

What three things does your operation need that you're not getting right now?

If you're having difficulty identifying larger projects you could initiate, ask your manager or your peers for some suggestions. Complete the following form to begin developing some project ideas. A sample is provided.

List two projects you would like to initiate.	Who else needs to be involved in the project?	Identify the four steps that will get the project started.
Develop a team housekeeping certification program that all teams would have to pass to be eligible for bonuses.	• *Other team leaders* • *Safety/Housekeeping coordinator from each team* • *Safety/Environmental engineer* • *Human resources manager*	*1. Collect data on the problem.* *2. Sell idea at plant council meeting.* *3. Charter task force.* *4. Benchmark with other companies.*

Now consider what would happen to your time if you actually started these two projects. Develop a time sheet (like the one on page 236) comparing how you spent your time as a new team leader with how it's spent as a mature team leader with a more project-focused role.

Week 2
Checking your changing role

For your transition to proceed as smoothly as possible, you need the support of your manager, the organization, and your teams. You can get that support by seeking their ideas on your new role.

1. **Interview your manager.**
   a. What direction is the organization taking with the team leader role?

   b. I have some ideas about how I could make a more proactive contribution (insert ideas from page 237). What do you think about these ideas?

   c. Are there other projects I should be involved in as a way to add value to the organization?

2. **Interview your team.**
   a. What kind of help do you still need from me?

   b. When, and how often, would you like to see me?

   c. What concerns would you have if I took a more externally focused, project-oriented role?

3. **Get agreement from the organization on the changing role of the leader.**

It may help to get all the leaders in your organization together to reach agreement on the new role of leaders. Consider using an agenda like the one below to facilitate consensus.

- Need for a change in the role
  —Teams' needs are changing
  —More value-added things we could get involved in (use organization's project list)

- Agreement on the new role
  —Percent of time on leader-initiated projects
  —Percent of time coaching teams
  —Percent of time on traditional duties

- Support needed from the organization
  —Training (project management, computer, etc.)
  —Time for new role
  —Removing potential barriers (access, information, treading on support departments' turf)

Use all the input you've gathered to develop a new role agreement with your manager. Fill in the following spaces to document the agreement.

What I will be doing less of:

What I will be doing more of:

How I will spend my time in the new role:

____ % working on projects I initiate

____ % working on projects assigned by the organization

____ % coaching teams

What I'm accountable for	How these will be measured	New skills I need	What help I need
Inventory reduction	*Increase inventory turns by 40 percent with cross-functional team*	*Project management*	*Support from manager: get me out of daily production meeting* *Support from team: take turns attending production meeting in my place*

When you get agreement on the basics of the new role with your manager, review it with your team.

Week 3
Branching out (developing lateral focus)

Most leaders of mature teams find that their interactions with other people will change, from simply funneling messages up and down the organization . . .

. . . to interactions in which they solve cross-department problems, implement sitewide solutions, and work with customers and suppliers.

Developing a Larger Focus

How much do you know about solving cross-department problems, implementing sitewide solutions, working with customers and suppliers, and more? All of these functions are part of what's expected of a mature team leader. There are several things you can do to develop a broader perspective. First, assess what you know now about these functions. List your organization's corporate departments, major suppliers, and major customers (not just the ones your teams interact with directly). Rate your familiarity with each one using this scale:

0 = no knowledge of function or problems

1 = could explain function to others

2 = detailed knowledge of inner workings

Department, customer, or supplier	Familiarity

Next, start branching out by setting up a meeting with a peer from one of the areas with which you are least familiar. Do the following:

1. Ask for a brief tour of the area.

2. Ask the other person about the problems and issues he or she faces.

   • What are the biggest problems in your area?

   • What problems does our department (our organization) cause for you?

   • What kinds of things cause you to have to delay the product/service? Rework the product/service? Scrap the product/service?

3. Offer to reciprocate with a tour and explanation of your area.

Potential Projects

Your discussions might turn up ideas for improvement in processes, communication, work flow, etc. As you complete your meetings, use this form to keep track of ideas for potential projects:

Common problems across areas:	People affected by the problems who might be willing to collaborate on a solution:
Other potential projects:	

Week 4
Helping your teams from a distance

As you start to focus more on projects, you might find that you have less frequent contact with your teams. This can become a problem unless you take some specific steps:

1. Discuss your changing role with team members.

2. Identify several ways to stay in touch with the teams.

3. Plan regular points of contact with the team.

1. **Discuss your changing role with team members.**

   Explain how your role is changing.

   - Shift to project focus
   - Cross-team problem solving

   Discuss how this change will benefit the teams.

   - More autonomy for team members

Reinforce why this change in roles is necessary.

- The team is becoming self-sufficient.
- There are still big problems to be solved in the organization.

Identify the teams' concerns.

Agree on what you can do to help.

2. **Identify several ways to stay in touch with the teams.**

   Other leaders have handled this issue by:

   - Establishing regular office hours to meet with team members.
   - Posting their daily schedule in a place where everyone can read it.
   - Starting or ending each day with a walk through the team area.

   Other ideas you have:

   List some ways you can tell when a problem is building in the team.

3. **Plan regular points of contact with the team.**

   Ask the team how often they would: (1) like to see you _____

                                        (2) need to see you _____

   How often will you attend team meetings?_____

   What will your role be in the meetings? (Check all that apply.)

   ☐ Update the team on your activities.

   ☐ Give the team feedback on how it's functioning.

   ☐ Help team members think through big problems.

   Other ideas you have:

Notes. . .

When to Call for Help

- If the leaders of teams can't agree on the new role, make sure that at least you and your manager agree on what you should be doing. Continue to work with the HR department, the design team, or the steering committee to develop some consistency in the leaders' role across the organization.

- If you and your manager can't agree on the new role, ask for an impartial facilitator you both respect.

If You Do Nothing Else . . .

1. Discuss the role transition with your team. Be sure everyone understands why it's necessary and what the implications will be for them.

2. Build the teams' confidence by providing support and encouragement. Show them how much they've progressed since they were formed.

3. Continue to identify larger projects that you will develop to add more value to the organization.

Month at a Glance

MONDAY	TUESDAY	WEDNESDAY	THURSDAY	FRIDAY	SATURDAY/SUNDAY
	Identify my own project ideas —2 hours	Interview my manager on organization's expectations —1 hour	Interview team on their expectations —1 hour		
Meet with all leaders; agree on new role —4 hours		Review changed role with team —1 hour			
	Meet with supplier to identify improvement projects —2 hours			Progress review meeting with manager —1 hour	
	Continue to coach members on new responsibilities —2 hours			Meet with team; agree on how to stay in touch —1 hour	

Time Budget

	Goal	Actual
Team coaching	40%	
Project work	30%	
Administrative	10%	
Personal development	20%	

Key Lessons

_____

_____

_____

_____

_____

Next Steps

_____

_____

_____

_____

_____

245

Mature Team Month 2

Notes. . .

Month 2

What to Expect

Getting accustomed to new roles is a long-term process, so don't be surprised if you and your teams still are trying to get adjusted to your new role. In fact, you might find yourself avoiding the new tasks and going back to the comfort of your more familiar team coaching role.

Your teams might be enabling this inertia. They might feel more comfortable having you around, even if they really don't need your day-to-day help anymore. In other words, you might find that you have to work deliberately at making the transition into your new role happen, while at the same time avoid getting sucked into the old routine.

Possible Concerns

My team members don't seem to value what I'm doing now. It seems they equate time away from the floor with wasted time.

If you think back to your own beliefs about what managers did (which is part of what you are doing now), you can understand why your team members might be suspicious.

Much of what you're doing now (thinking, planning, meeting with others) is hard to observe. The output probably isn't as readily apparent as the output of your teams' work.

Most of their doubts arise from a lack of understanding. Discuss what you're doing from the standpoint of return on investment (that is, taking two months to reengineer the distribution process will save the organization $350,000, or taking six months to work with a supplier on a networked computer system will reduce inventory by 23 percent and save $1.5 million in the first year).

I'm doing some tasks that no one in the organization has ever done before. What's to prevent management from deciding that I'm expendable? (In other words, if no one did it before, do we really need someone doing it now?)

Consider the alternative: Many of your old tasks are either no longer necessary (supervising others' work) or are being done by the team (running team meetings). Everyone's role in the organization must continue to evolve as non-value-added activities are worked out of the process and as customers' requirements change. Remaining the same in a changing organization probably is the fastest ticket out.

If you have doubts that what you are working on is truly valued by the organization, ask. Check with your manager. Offer alternative projects. Discuss the return that could be expected from each alternative. Then keep the management team informed of your progress and results.

Your Focus This Month

During the second month of the Mature Team Phase, you need to focus your attention on:

- Doing an environment scan.

- Reassessing your own training needs.

- Creating teamwork between your teams and their external customers and suppliers.

- Getting the organization's approval for new initiatives.

Week 1
Doing an environment scan

Your organization should be adapting continually to the demands of the external environment (customer needs, competition's changes, technological advances). Therefore, one of the best sources for improvement ideas is an assessment of the needs of key external stakeholders. Follow this three-step process to conduct this assessment, using the chart on page 249.

Step 1

List the key stakeholders outside your organization in column one in the chart.

Step 2

In column two identify what the external stakeholders need from your organization. Focus on what they need from you today and their expectations three to five years from now. Although the best way to obtain this information is in face-to-face interviews, you also can get a lot of the information you need over the phone. Be sure to coordinate with other leaders so as not to overwhelm the stakeholders with contacts.

Step 3

Identify what your organization needs from each external stakeholder in column three. You can do this by interviewing the person or group in your organization that has the most contact with the outside group (that is, sales or marketing reps for competitive information). Remember to include not only what your organization needs from the external group now, but also what it will need in the future.

Conflicting or Ambiguous Expectations

When you compare columns two and three, you are bound to find conflicts between the expectations (such as the "more lead time"/"less lead time" example). You may also find ambiguities. (We're not sure what they need!) Both conflicts and ambiguities are great starting points for improvement projects. Summarize any conflicting or ambiguous expectations, then write out an improvement idea. Following are two examples.

1. *ABC Supply Company wants more lead time; we want less.*

Improvement idea: Give them real-time computer access to our production schedule in return for shaving two days off the delivery schedule.

2. *No state employment service job candidate gets hired at our company; they don't understand our job requirements.*

Improvement idea: Invite state employment service reps to our facility, discuss job requirements, and have them do all our prescreening for us.

1. External Stakeholders	2. What They Need From Us	3. What We Need From Them	4. Improvement Ideas
Customers (top three)			
Competitors			
Home office (key contacts)			
Local community (key groups)			
Government agencies			
Suppliers (top five)			
Labor groups			

Fill in your own examples. Use these to propose improvement projects you will work on in your new role.

Week 2
Reassessing your own training needs

Most leaders need to focus on refining three sets of skills as their teams mature:

1. A refresher on foundation skills

2. New leadership skills

3. New technical skills

Assess your development needs in the following exercise. For each statement circle the number that best describes you. For each area add the numbers you circled and divide by three to determine your average for that area. Write this average next to "Skill Total."

Foundation Skills

	Never	Seldom	Sometimes	Often	Always

Coaching

	Never	Seldom	Sometimes	Often	Always
1. I provide coaching to others *before* major events.	1	2	3	4	5
2. People outside my teams ask me for coaching help.	1	2	3	4	5
3. I offer my thoughts, feelings, and rationale.	1	2	3	4	5

Skill Total_____

Encouraging Initiative

	Never	Seldom	Sometimes	Often	Always
1. I provide support without removing responsibility for action.	1	2	3	4	5
2. Each of my team members is working on an improvement idea.	1	2	3	4	5
3. I encourage team members to develop their skills, knowledge, and creativity.	1	2	3	4	5

Skill Total_____

Reinforcing Effective Performance	Never	Seldom	Sometimes	Often	Always
1. I go out of my way to reinforce at least one person each day.	1	2	3	4	5
2. In the organization I'm thought of as a leader who uses reinforcement a lot.	1	2	3	4	5
3. I feel natural and sincere when reinforcing others.	1	2	3	4	5

Skill Total_____

New Leadership Skills

Advancing Teams

	Never	Seldom	Sometimes	Often	Always
1. I recognize signs of ineffective team dynamics.	1	2	3	4	5
2. I fix ineffective dynamics in my teams.	1	2	3	4	5
3. I have a plan to help my teams advance to the next level.	1	2	3	4	5

Skill Total_____

Building Business Partnerships

	Never	Seldom	Sometimes	Often	Always
1. I work to break down the barriers that hamper efforts to negotiate, collaborate, and communicate between areas.	1	2	3	4	5
2. I work with my internal and external partners to achieve shared goals.	1	2	3	4	5
3. I work with other people in a spirit of partnership to achieve win-win results for all.	1	2	3	4	5

Skill Total_____

New Technical Skills

	Never	Seldom	Sometimes	Often	Always

Project Management

	Never	Seldom	Sometimes	Often	Always
1. I complete projects on time and within budget.	1	2	3	4	5
2. I involve all the right people at the right time.	1	2	3	4	5
3. My project ideas are fully and successfully implemented.	1	2	3	4	5

Skill Total_____

Business Analysis

	Never	Seldom	Sometimes	Often	Always
1. I understand our strengths and weaknesses compared to our competitors'.	1	2	3	4	5
2. I am up to date on how our customer requirements are changing.	1	2	3	4	5
3. I understand our organization's financial performance.	1	2	3	4	5

Skill Total_____

Evaluating Your Development Needs

Transfer your rating for each skill into the column next to that skill. For instance, if your Skill Total for Coaching was 3, write 3 in the Scores column opposite Coaching. Then circle any skill area with 3 or less. You will want to plan some additional training around these skills. Possible activities are provided; write some of your own in the space provided.

Development Activities	Scores	Possible Activities

Foundation skills
  Coaching
  Encouraging Initiative
  Reinforcing Effective Performance
 	
New leadership skills
  Advancing Teams
  Building Business Partnerships
 	
New technical skills
  Project Management
  Business Analysis
		☐ Attend training.
		
		☐ Find a mentor.
		
		☐ Ask to be assigned to a project with someone who does this well.
		
		☐ Read a book about the subject.
		
		☐ Ask for additional feedback from team, peers, manager.

Week 3
Developing external partnerships

If you've done a good job of designing teams in your organization, you probably have broken down most of the internal hand-offs and boundaries. Now all that remains is to break down the walls separating your teams from their external customers and suppliers.

As organizations attempt to provide service better, faster, and cheaper, the boundaries between organizations are becoming increasingly blurred. Suppliers permanently station people at their customers' sites to ensure satisfaction with delivery and service. Customers want to create joint product development and problem-solving teams. It's getting difficult to tell where one organization ends and another begins. Your teams can benefit from this trend by exploring new forms of contact with customers and suppliers.

If you're still not convinced, list your major external customers and suppliers below. Then, with your teams' help, identify the problems and issues you have not been able to resolve with them so far.

External Customers

Ongoing Problems/Issues

External Suppliers

Ongoing Problem/Issues

With your teams' help, identify what forms of increased contact and communication might be appropriate for each customer and supplier. Start with the low-contact possibilities and work up to the more intensive, high-contact types of communication efforts.

**Link the Customers and Suppliers
with the Appropriate Form of Contact**

Low Contact

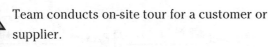

Team conducts on-site tour for a customer or supplier.

Your team members have the phone numbers for key customers or suppliers.

Customers or suppliers are on the same e-mail or voice mail system as team members.

Customer or supplier personnel attend team meetings.

Your team identifies one problem a quarter to solve with customer or supplier and creates a cross-organization problem-solving team.

Customer or supplier member becomes a full-time team member.

Team moves on-site with customer or supplier for one week a month.

High Contact

Set a goal with your teams to reduce or eliminate problems with each of your key customers and suppliers through a plan of increased contact. You might expect, for example, to eliminate 50 percent of the problems you've listed on page 254 by the end of the year.

If your team has had very little contact with customers or suppliers, you might want to start slowly with one customer or supplier at a low to medium level of contact.

Week 4
Getting organizational approval

Before proceeding with any major, new initiatives, it's best to have official sanction. This is one circumstance in which you're better off asking for permission now than asking for forgiveness later! The consequences of going ahead without the key players informed and on-board include:

- Second-guessing your process or solution.

- Stalling the implementation of your improvement.

- Overlooking an important perspective or source of information.

For each new project or initiative you're considering, identify the key internal stakeholders below by answering these questions:

- Who would be affected by the idea or project?

- Who would expect to be involved or informed?

- Who controls the resources I need to complete the project?

- Who would have to approve the expenditure of resources?

- Who could contribute?

	Project _____	Project _____	Project _____
Who would be affected?			
Who should be involved/informed?			
Who controls needed resources?			
Who approves expenditures?			
Who could contribute?			

To sell your manager or a larger management group on a project or an idea, it might be helpful to organize your presentation in the following way. (A sample is provided.)

Presentation Outline	Sample	Your Project or Idea
Background: The circumstances that caused you to consider the project or idea.	*Last Friday I had to give three visitors and two patients directions in the hallways to find a hospital department.*	
Problem: The extent and cost of the problem.	*"Hard to find my way around" was the number two cause of guest dissatisfaction.*	
Consequences: What would happen if nothing was done to fix the problem.	*Continue to lose patients to the smaller Memorial Hospital, which is perceived to have a friendlier atmosphere.*	
Benefits: How will you, other managers, and the organization benefit if the problem is fixed?	*Increased guest satisfaction. Reduced delays from lost patients. Less personal time spent escorting visitors through hospital.*	

Be sure to determine in advance what you're asking for:

☐ Approval for you to spend time developing a more complete proposal.

☐ Approval for you to research the problem and come back with recommended solutions.

☐ The resources you need to implement the improvement idea.

If you have any doubts, you might want to document the agreements in a memo.

When to Call for Help

- You have an idea for a project that you know is the right thing to do, but you know that some managers will strongly resist it. Ask someone you respect to help you think through the introduction of the idea.

- You've taken all the training that your company has to offer, yet you still need development in several areas. Ask your training or human resources department to help you identify external opportunities for training that address your specific needs.

If You Do Nothing Else . . .

1. Initiate at least one project that affects more than just your teams.

2. Start working on one of your own development needs.

3. Check with your teams to make sure they're receiving enough support from you.

Month at a Glance

MONDAY	TUESDAY	WEDNESDAY	THURSDAY	FRIDAY	SATURDAY/ SUNDAY
Plan environment scan —2 hours		Call supplier contact —1 hour		Put together initial project plan —2 hours	
Assess skills —1 hour	Plan development activities —1 hour			Progress review meeting with manager —1 hour	
		Agree with team on next step in customer contact —2 hours			
			Sell project idea to Admin Council —1 hour		

Time Budget

	Goal	Actual
Team coaching	35%	
Project work	35%	
Administrative	10%	
Personal development	20%	

Key Lessons

_____

_____

_____

_____

_____

_____

Next Steps

_____

_____

_____

_____

_____

_____

Mature Team Month 3

Notes. . .

Month 3

What To Expect

By now you and your teams should be getting more comfortable with your new roles. The teams should be able to handle issues in your absence. They probably are having fewer crises and are involving you less in day-to-day team issues.

You should be immersed in one or more new projects or assignments. You might be discovering that getting things done at the organizational level isn't as easy as it might have appeared. But you'll need to resist the temptation to work on your own. While it might seem easier in the short term, in the long run it will make implementation of your ideas much more difficult.

Possible Concerns

I can't believe it, but the person I'm having the most difficulty with is my manager. Even after we agreed that I would pick up five responsibilities from her plate, she's still not turning them over. When I ask her about it, she has all kinds of excuses, such as, "Well, I just haven't had time to get it ready for you yet," and, "Oh yeah, I forgot. I'll get to it next week." Now what do I do?

Don't give up. Remain gently persistent. Make it as easy as possible for her to turn the responsibilities over to you. Think back to when you were faced with turning over responsibilities to the teams. It was hard to figure out where to start and how to communicate everything they needed to know about the task.

Offer to help her the next time she compiles the quarterly report. Volunteer to do a small but specific part of a larger task. Suggest a first step you would be willing to take on. Be sure that you build in opportunities for her to review your work before it goes out.

I know my teams are supposed to be adjusting to this new arrangement, but they actually seem to have regressed! They're doing some really juvenile stuff now, which I haven't seen for over a year. Last week some team members scrawled nasty messages on pieces of paper, folded them into airplanes, and flew them into another team's area.

This "acting out" behavior is probably a crude attempt to get your attention while testing the limits of their new autonomy. Don't overreact. It will only reinforce their dependence on you. Do check to be sure that you're giving the team enough positive attention in the form of coaching and reinforcement. If the behavior continues, analyze the problem as a group.

Your Focus This Month

This month you will focus on:

- Identifying cross-team projects.

- Assessing your initiative.

- Touching base with your manager.

- Turning over final responsibilities to the teams.

Week 1

Identifying cross-team projects

In most organizations there are common problems that plague several teams. Unfortunately, each team attacks the problem in its own way, diluting or even negating the impact of the individual efforts. What you need is a coordinated plan of attack, focusing on the 20 percent of your shared problems that create 80 percent of the headaches. To do this you'll need to involve leaders or members from other teams.

Steps	Examples	Your Organization
1. Start by generating a list of shared services or processes. Ask the group to fill in the blanks: "We all use the_____." "We all are affected by the_____."	*Cafeteria; maintenance* *Purchasing system; computer system*	
2. Narrow the list by eliminating areas that are beyond your control or ability to influence.	*New OSHA regulations; corporate smoking policy*	
3. Then ask the group to classify the remaining items in the following grid.		

Amount of Aggravation Caused — grid with quadrants labeled 2, 1 (top) and 4, 3 (bottom). Vertical axis LO to HI. Horizontal axis: Ease of Fix, LO to HI.

Amount of Aggravation Caused — grid with quadrants: (top-left) • Standard reports • Team budget process; (top-right) Safety gear; (bottom-left) Documentation of SOPs; (bottom-right) • Forklift training • Outside travel service. Vertical axis LO to HI. Horizontal axis: Ease of Fix, LO to HI.

Amount of Aggravation Caused — blank grid. Vertical axis LO to HI. Horizontal axis: Ease of Fix, LO to HI.

Usually, you will start with projects in quadrant 1 (very aggravating, but easy to fix) and then tackle projects in quadrants 2 and 3. Representatives from the different teams might want to take responsibility for leading various projects. Others from the group who feel strongly about the issue may volunteer to participate on the problem-solving team. Use the following form to list your best potential projects and to identify leaders to take responsibility for the project and others who would like to be involved.

Best Potential Projects	Lead	Others Who Would Like To Be Involved

Week 2
Assessing your initiative

As you take on increased responsibilites, you'll need to demonstrate a high degree of initiative: taking action beyond explicit job responsibilities and originating action rather than responding only to the actions of others. In this phase of team development, you'll not only initiate the role change by seeking new responsibilities, but you'll take on tasks that demand more initiative (such as selling an idea, persuading others to be involved, gathering data, contacting people outside the organization, etc.). Although people rarely are disciplined for lacking initiative, initiative is almost always mentioned as a prerequisite for job success at all levels.

To check how you're doing on this expanded dimension of your job, complete the following self-assessment:

I . . .	Routinely	Sometimes	Rarely
Actively seek solutions to problems before being asked or directed.			
Initiate self-development efforts.			
Try easier, more effective ways to do the job.			
Generate ideas for projects.			
Take action without consulting others.			
Do more than required.			
Collect extra information that might be useful for reports or meetings.			
Volunteer to help others when my work load is light.			
Volunteer to serve on committees and task forces.			
Challenge biases and preconceived beliefs.			
Seek ideas from other fields to incorporate in team efforts.			

Scoring

Give yourself . . .

0   points for every time you checked "Rarely."

1   point for every time you checked "Sometimes."

2   points for every time you checked "Routinely."

If your points fall between . . .

0-6   You are a slug. If you don't get moving, the rest of the organization is likely to run you over.

7-13   You are moving in the right direction. You just need to crank up your efforts a notch or two.

14-22   You are already moving full speed ahead.

Ideas for Developing Your Initiative

- Select one of the items from the assessment that you currently do rarely and set a goal to do it five times in one week.

- Maintain a list or computer file of new ideas, even if they are not immediately usable.

- Read widely and regularly, even outside of your field of interest.

- Observe people with high initiative at work; identify one or two behaviors.

- Set aside quiet time each week to plan improvements or initiate new projects.

Week 3
Checkpoint #6: Touching base with your manager

Don't go too far into this role transition without checking to make sure you and your manager are on the same wavelength. This may be even more important now than it was in earlier stages, because with mature teams:

- Leaders' roles are not as well defined.

- There typically isn't as much organizational attention and support as when teams were first getting started.

Plan a progress review meeting with your manager, using the framework below. A completed sample is provided on the next page.

How I'm doing against my goals: **How I'm spending my time:**		How the teams are doing against their goals:			
			Goal 1:	Goal 2:	Goal 3:
		Team			
		Team			

Project Update			
Projects underway	**Where in schedule?**	**Problems**	**Solutions** **(Your own? Your manager's?)**
Things I need from my manager:		**Things my manager needs from me:**	

Overall Progress	How the teams are doing against their goals:		
How I'm doing against my goals:		*Cost*	*Schedule*	*Customer satisfaction*

How I'm doing against my goals:
Service levels are ahead of plan, team development on track, new product launch behind schedule.

How I'm spending my time:
30 percent with teams, 35 percent with launch team, 10 percent on revamping proposal process, 10 percent on personal development, 15 percent meetings/administration.

How the teams are doing against their goals:	*Cost*	*Schedule*	*Customer satisfaction*
Team A	*Ahead of goal*	*On track*	*Ahead*
Team B	*On track*	*On track*	*Behind*

Project Update

Projects underway	Where in schedule?	Problems	Solutions (Your own? Your manager's?)
LT launch	*Still in design phase (two weeks behind)*	*Sales & marketing bickering over specs*	*Bring team together to refocus on vision* *Get sales & marketing to agree on superordinate goal*
New proposal process	*In implementation (two days ahead)*		
Local area network	*Implemented: in monitoring*	*Taking too long to get new hires trained*	*Give one member on each team training responsibility*

Things I need from my manager:
- *Permission to get out of monthly administration meeting—send Jane instead*
- *Feedback on project management skills*

Things my manager needs from me:

Week 4
Turning over final responsibilities to the teams

Even with teams that have been working together for more than a year, there often are some sophisticated tasks they haven't tackled yet. Some of the most common include:

- Hiring team members.

- Preparing a team budget.

- Setting team goals.

- Reviewing fellow team members' performance.

- Disciplining team members.

- Determining team members' compensation.

Note other responsibilities from your organization:

Evaluate each of these responsibilities against the following checklist:

☐ It would be possible to turn this responsibility over to the team (i.e., the steering committee or the union contract has not deemed the responsibility off-limits).

☐ It would help the team feel more like it was running its own small business.

☐ It would help the team control more of its own variances.

☐ Some team members have expressed a willingness to take on more responsibility.

☐ We could provide the training the team needs to handle the responsibility.

Once you have evaluated each of the responsibilities against these criteria, you can use the worksheet on the facing page to plan if or how to transfer them to the team.

WARNING: It is not necessary or right to turn all of these responsibilities over to the teams.

Remaining Responsibilities	Team Will Never Do	Team Could Do Later	Team Could Do Now	Training They Need	Training They Need	Other Support They Need
Hiring team members (from outside the organization)			✔	*Training in interviewing skills* *Observe another team's data integration session*	*Legal requirements*	*Human resources representative to participate in first two hires*

Notes. . .

Month 3

When to Call for Help

If the team is ready and willing to take on more responsibility but others are resistant (other leaders, your manager, support departments, etc.), try enlisting more support from other sources. Sometimes the team members or the design team can be very influential.

If You Do Nothing Else . . .

1. Evaluate additional responsibilities for possible transfer to the teams.

2. Find a team accomplishment to celebrate.

3. Evaluate your initiative.

Month at a Glance

MONDAY	TUESDAY	WEDNESDAY	THURSDAY	FRIDAY	SATURDAY/ SUNDAY
		Convene team leaders; start joint project —2 hours			
Self-assess initiative —1 hour				Mini Team Celebration —15 minutes	
	Evaluate strategy for broadening my business perspective —1/2 hour		Meet with manager		
	Review remaining responsibilities with teams —2 hours		Coach team members to take on additional responsibilities —2 hours		

Time Budget

	Goal	Actual
Team coaching	35%	
Project work	40%	
Administrative	10%	
Personal development	15%	

Key Lessons

_____
_____
_____
_____
_____
_____
_____

Next Steps

_____
_____
_____
_____
_____
_____
_____

Mature Team Month 4

Notes. . .

Month 4

What to Expect

If everything is falling into place, you should feel that you're making a substantial contribution to the business. The projects that you are involved in should be giving you a whole new perspective on the business.

Possible Concerns

Okay, I finally have my manager and my teams cooperating with this role transition. Now I'm bumping into resistance from support departments. Purchasing seems to regard any contact with suppliers as their domain.

Think back to the techniques you used with resistors on the team. Remember that resistance often stems from lack of understanding or lack of involvement. Consider employing the following techniques with the support departments:

☐ Involve them in shaping the project idea; ask for their help and input.

☐ Take time to understand their perspectives, problems, and motivations; find out what would make their lives easier.

☐ Explain the project or idea in terms of what's in it for them.

☐ Share credit with them.

☐ If all else fails, report them to your manager (just kidding).

Your Focus This Month

This month you will focus on:

- Assessing your project management skills.

- Evaluating projects by conducting cost-benefits analyses.

- Developing proposals for new business.

- Assessing your personal progress.

Week 1

Assessing your project management skills

Many leaders of teams have discovered that managing a project requires a different twist on the leadership skills they used to manage a permanent intact team. Some of the differences include:

- ☐ Greater reliance on influence rather than position power.

- ☐ More planning and thinking rather than "doing."

- ☐ The need to sell and resell the project concept and process.

Now that you are embroiled in one or more projects, assess how well you are doing. Circle the number on the continuum that best describes your progress in:

Selling the idea to key stakeholders.

5	4	3	2	1

All key stakeholders are committed.   Only 1 or 2 key stakeholders are committed.

Involving the right people in planning.

5	4	3	2	1

All stakeholders felt they had sufficient input.   Several important people were overlooked.

Communicating progress to key stakeholders.

5	4	3	2	1

Stakeholders receive regular updates.   Stakeholders have to ask for information.

Following up on commitments.

5	4	3	2	1

All promises have been kept. | | | Several important balls have been dropped.

Keeping the project on schedule.

5	4	3	2	1

No deadlines have been missed. | | | There is no project schedule.

Managing personal time on the project.

5	4	3	2	1

I still have plenty of time to handle my other responsibilities. | | | I spend much more time on the project than I had planned.

Acknowledging and dealing with problems (rather than avoiding or denying them).

5	4	3	2	1

All major problems are openly discussed and solved in project team meetings. | | | There is tension and complaining, but nothing is being done about it.

Scoring

Add the numbers you circled for each item. If your total was:

28 or more   You are either a very effective project manager or you are deluding yourself.

18–27   You should work on your one or two lowest items; ask for help and feedback.

17 or less   You need serious project management training or coaching.

Week 2
Cost-benefit analysis

Persuading managers to try something new usually requires some justification—often in economic terms. For this reason, leaders of mature teams need to become proficient at cost-benefit analysis. This also might be referred to as return on investment (ROI). For example, the investment (cost) of a computer training program might be $85,000 over two years, and the expected return (benefit) is $170,000 over the three-year life cycle, resulting in an ROI of two (meaning that you're getting back twice what you invested).

Example

To illustrate, suppose you're interested in automating some of the regular reports that must be submitted to your corporate office. You and the other team leaders each spend an average of nine hours a month completing the reports, which don't directly add value to the customers. Because they can't be eliminated (you've checked), you've determined that a team member could handle the responsibility in less time if the process was more automated. To sell this idea to management, you must first estimate the costs of developing a computer program to streamline the process. One way to do this is shown below:

	Personnel	Facilities	Equipment	Material
Analysis	$200			
Design	$1,200			
Development	$8,000		$500	
Implementation	$5,000		$800	$2,500
Maintenance	$1,000			

Total = $19,200

Working with your organization's information technology group, you determine that most costs will be associated with the software development. You also estimate the ongoing costs of maintaining the new system. Now you have to estimate the benefits from the new system. The benefits generally fall in three categories:

reducing existing costs.

avoiding certain future costs (such as the need to hire more people).

doing something faster, better, cheaper, etc.

In our example, it currently requires nine hours of each team leader's time a month (9 hours multiplied by 32 team leaders, multiplied by the average salary of $18/hour, multiplied by 12 months equals $62,208). Under the new system, one team member can generate the same report in one-half hour a month (.5 hours multiplied by 64 team members, multiplied by the average salary of $12/hour, multiplied by 12 months equals $4,608). Thus, the cost reduction is $57,600 ($62,208 minus $4,608); and the ROI is three ($57,600 divided by $19,200) in the first year alone. Not bad!

Use this example to work through a cost-benefit analysis of one of your project ideas.

Week 3
Developing proposals for new business

Rather than settling for dividing up the same old pie (or worse yet, carving up shares of a dwindling pie), many leaders of mature teams set out to expand the pie by bringing in new business.

Where do these ideas for new business come from?

- Suggestions from customers: new needs, variations on existing products/services, something they can't get from you or your competitors.

- Benchmarking other organizations: Some hospitals got the idea of a patient-care mobile from observing local "bookmobiles."

- Ideas from competitors: A competitor introduces a "user guide" for its products; you set up "user conferences."

- Unexpected successes or failures: There often is unanticipated demand for part of a product (for instance, customers inquiring about the packaging instead of the product), or demand from unexpected segments of the market that could lead to a niche product or service.

- Changes in market or customer demographics: These could involve changes in the age of customers, new overseas markets, etc.

- Complementary products or services: Ideas for dispensers, job aids, training materials, or service agreements often can become new product lines.

Most leaders aren't short on ideas, they just don't know how to package the idea for management.

It isn't hard if you treat this as if you were making a proposal to a group of backers for a small business start-up.

Step	Example	Your idea

1. Research the market:
  • Discuss with customers.
 	
  • Check competition.
  • Gauge price sensitivity.
	
	• *Customers complain about not having a way to organize all the product documentation.*
	• *No competitors offer desk reference sets.*
	• *Customers would be willing to pay $59.95 for desk reference set.*	

2. Identify stakeholders:
  • Sell to person in your organization who benefits the most.
  • Make an informal presentation.
 	
  • Identify issues/concerns.
	
	• *Sales VP has the most to gain.*
	
	• *Make cocktail napkin presentation to sales VP at next sales meeting.*
	• *His only concern is pricing—check this with 20 more customers.*	

3. Prepare a business plan, including:
  • Executive summary.
  • Product/Service improvement idea.
  • Marketing/Sales plan.
 	
  • Operations plan.
  • Summary of risks.
  • Financial analysis.
 	
  • Implementation plan.
	
	• *Describe how desk reference set fits with our mission.*
	• *Describe the set, its use and benefits.*
	• *Document size of market, competition, pricing, sales strategy.*
	• *Estimate requirements for producing the desk set.*
	• *Describe market threat.*
	• *Document cost to produce ($32.95) versus price ($59.95).*
	• *Outline production, marketing, sales timetables.*	

4. Present the plan: • Identify a sponsor to help with resources and any internal politics.	 • *Pat Hill (sales VP) will oversee the project.*	

If you need more help, Gifford Pinchot's book *Intrapreneuring* is an excellent source for tips on developing new business ideas within your current organization.

Week 4
Taking stock of your own progress

If only team leaders could have before and after snapshots of their own development! No doubt they'd be quite surprised—and pleased.

You need to maintain your own perspective on the transformation you've been through. Compare your before-teams state to your current state, using the chart to the right.

	Where You Were Before Teams	Where You Are Now
Leadership Style • What employees say about you • How you feel about your style		
Skills • What you can do: —technically —interpersonally —administratively		
Knowledge • Of the business • Of customers • Of leadership • Of teams		
Value to the Organization 1= Babysitting (watching, controlling others) 5= Business leader		

Because you can't always count on getting reinforcement from your manager, the organization, or even your teams, many successful leaders find ways of celebrating their own progress:

☐ Treat yourself to something you truly enjoy (a site visit, a lunch with other team leaders, etc.).

☐ Chart your progress (keep a list of new skills, new areas of knowledge, etc.).

☐ Brag about an accomplishment to a friend (a fellow team leader, your brother, your mother).

☐ Revel in the natural rewards of the new role (increased freedom, responsibility, personal development, and impact on the business.

You've come a long way since those first days with teams. You deserve to revel in your progress!

Notes. . .

Month 4

When for Call for Help

If you're having trouble developing your new business proposal, seek help from experts in the areas in which you're stuck (for instance, marketing, finance, sales). Most people are flattered when you ask for their help.

If You Do Nothing Else . . .

1. Check with the teams to make sure they're on track and getting the support they need.

2. Take time out to evaluate your progress over the last year and a half.

3. Reward yourself.

Month at a Glance

MONDAY	TUESDAY	WEDNESDAY	THURSDAY	FRIDAY	SATURDAY/ SUNDAY
	Assess project management skills —1 hour			Update meetings with teams —2 hours	
		Draft cost-benefits analysis —2 hours	Review analysis with accounting, get feedback —1 hour		
				Start developing new business proposal —3 hours	
	Take stock of personal progress —2 hours	Schedule rewarding activity —1 hour			

Time Budget

	Goal	Actual
Team coaching	30%	
Project work	45%	
Administrative	10%	
Personal development	15%	

Key Lessons

_____

_____

_____

_____

_____

_____

Next Steps

_____

_____

_____

_____

_____

_____

_____

Other Sources of Help

Books About Teams

All Teams Are Not Created Equal (Ketchum, L. D. & Trist, E.; Newbury Park, CA: Sage Publications, 1992; 318 pp.) provides a wealth of savvy advice for plant start-up and retrofit teams. The center-out model offers a top-notch strategy for leaders involved with teams that strive for long-lasting change. The book also offers six classes of manager behavior, from embracing to sabotaging change, and ideas that enable leaders to increase their effectiveness.

Business Without Bosses (Manz, C. C. & Sims, H. P.; New York: John Wiley & Sons, 1993; 238 pp.) offers team leaders and managers valuable ideas about their roles and how to implement teams successfully. Subjects include day-to-day team experiences and the good and the bad of teams.

Empowered Teams (Wellins, R. S., Byham, W. C., & Wilson, J. M.; San Francisco: Jossey-Bass, 1991; 258 pp.) outlines how to implement self-directed teams successfully. It explains how self-directed teams work, how they're different from other teams, and what they do on a day-to-day basis. It covers the key factors for successful implementation taken from a wide variety of companies, private and public, large and small, that are using self-directed work teams. Most of all, it provides practical hands-on advice for working through the stages of building strong teams.

Inside Teams (Wellins, R. S., Byham, W. C., & Dixon, G. R.; San Francisco: Jossey-Bass, 1994; 390 pp.) offers a behind-the-scenes look at how 20 of the world's best team-based companies realized results through teamwork. Each case history chronicles why teams were chosen as a competitive strategy, how teams started, the problems encountered, the lessons learned, and the dramatic impact teams had on the organization's bottom line.

Succeeding as a Self-directed Work Team (Harper, B. & Harper, A.; Croton-on-Hudson, NY: MW Corporation, 1989; 103 pp.) asks and answers 20 common questions about teams. It is a good introduction to the concept and is presented in an easy-to-read format. The book answers questions of interest to team members (for instance, What are the benefits for team members? and, Can anyone learn to be an effective team member?) and leaders (for instance, How is leadership handled by the SDWT? and, What is the new role of the manager and supervisor?).

Succeeding With Teams (Wellins, R. S., Schaaf, D., & Shomo, K. H.; Minneapolis: Lakewood Books, 1994; 126 pp.) is a handbook for teams at all stages of development. Each chapter offers 10 tips with explanations, suggestions, and, in some cases, applications of how they've worked for other organizations.

Books That Help With Your Expanding Role

Intrapreneuring (Pinchot, G.; New York: Harper & Row, 1985; 368 pp.) is extremely helpful to team leaders who are taking on a strategic role. It provides excellent advice on developing business ideas and initiating projects within an organization.

Leadership Trapeze (Wilson, J. M., George, J., Wellins, R. S., & Byham, W. C.; San Francisco: Jossey-Bass, 1994; 279 pp.) offers strategies for leading in a team setting. Interviews with managers and leaders of self-directed teams help illustrate the changes in behavior required to master the skills of leadership.

Process Consultation (Schein, E. H.; Reading, MA: Addison-Wesley, 1988; 204 pp.) is a good introduction for leaders who want to get better at the internal consulting aspect of their role. The book (Volume 1 in the Addison-Wesley Organization Development Series) not only helps leaders understand how groups work, but it provides helpful suggestions on diagnosis intervention and coaching.

Research Studies

Barry Macy completed a large-scale analysis of more than 130 organizations with employee involvement efforts titled "Organizational Design and Work Innovations: Impacts 1961-1991." It was published in Research in Organizational Change and Development (Vol. VII, Woodman, R. W. and Pasmore, W. A., eds., JAI Press, 1993).

John Cotter conducted a similar survey of organizations that moved to teams in seven countries, which first appeared as "Designing Organizations that Work: An Open Socio-technical Systems Perspective." Copies of the study can be obtained from John J. Cotter Associates in Studio City, California.

About Development Dimensions International

Development Dimensions International (DDI) is a leading provider of human resource programs and services designed to create high-involvement organizations. Founded in 1970, DDI now provides services to more than 9,000 clients around the world, spanning a diverse range of industries and including more than 400 of the Fortune 500 corporations.

DDI's products and services fall into three general areas:

1. Assessment and selection: ensures that organizations select and promote team members and leaders most capable of working in high-involvement organizations.

2. Organizational change: involves a wide range of consulting services and expertise in implementing teams.

3. Training and development: includes proven and comprehensive skill-building systems for teams and their leaders.

For more information, write or call:

Development Dimensions International
World Headquarters—Pittsburgh
1225 Washington Pike
Bridgeville, PA 15017-2838
800-933-4624

About the Authors

Jeanne Wilson and Jill George live, eat, and breathe teams. As coleaders of DDI's team practice, they consult with clients on team visioning, work redesign, leader assessment and development, and team performance management. Some of the their recent projects include:

- Implementing self-directed teams of sales and service professionals for Buick.

- Redesigning the work flow and team boundaries at UCAR Carbon's R&D facility.

- Developing a joint union/management team implementation at several sites within Union Pacific Railroad.

- Designing a team performance management system with Miller Brewing and Henkel/Emery.

Jeanne and Jill are coauthors of *The Leadership Trapeze* (1994, with Richard S. Wellins and William C. Byham) and co-developed DDI's Changing Role of the Supervisor program. Their last adventure in team consulting involved a goat, a mango, and a golden egg! (Don't ask.)

Index

With Hearty Thanks . . .

We would like to thank the people who turned this guide from an idea on a napkin into a final product:

- Bill Byham and Rich Wellins encouraged us and believed in our "idear" (usually pronounced idea).

- Mike "You Want It When?" Crawmer honed the fine detail and provided sustaining humor for the project.

- Alan Cheney of Air Products and Lee Kricher provided savvy and often entertaining review comments.

- Ellen Wellins mastered the fine art of tag team editing.

- David Biber created the delightful cartoons.

- Shelby Gracey helped us get organized at the outset and processed mass quantities of verbiage.

- Mark Mosko provided the styling, formatting, and graphics. Thanks for your staying power.

- Anne Maers–for her faith in our project as evidenced by the 200 sales before we even got it off the cocktail napkin!

- Andrea "Eagle Eye" Garry proofread the entire guide.

Printed on recycled paper as part of DDI's concern for the environment.